Best Wishes

Roy Jones '16

1

The Pawnbrokers

The Fall And Rise Of The Pawnbroking Profession

RAY PERRY

To Sharon, Sabrina and Jay.

ISBN:1530021103
ISBN-13: 978-1530021109

About the Author

Ray Perry was Chief Executive of the National Pawnbrokers Association (NPA) from late 2011 to 2016, representing over 2000 stores and 95% of the UK market. He worked with the treasury and Financial Conduct Authority (FCA) to help shape the new Consumer Credit regime. On a daily basis he dealt with senior politicians and legislators, pawnbrokers, customers and the media. Prior to this Ray was Executive Director of the Chartered Institute of Management Accountants (CIMA) and Marketing Director of the Chartered Institute of Marketing (CIM) and Chief Executive of their resources centre. He is a Henley MBA holder.

As Chief Executive of the National Pawnbroking Association he met key stakeholders and business leaders in the sector and has studied the Pawnbrokers archives. He is an expert in the field.

His previous works include;

Marketing Unwrapped- 2000- Wiley & Sons

Various white papers for CIMA, CIM and NPA

He wrote a column for several years in the Sunday Times Business Section as a consultant on the Small Business Panel in the 1990s

The Author Ray Perry

Contents

Appendix

Chapter 1 Introduction

The Pawnbroker has always been there at the heart of society and yet as we shall see in later chapters, has remained largely invisible for the last 1000 years.

The Chinese were pawning their goods 3000 years ago, not least for ship building, wars, and exploration. Much later Queen Isabella of Spain pawned her jewellery to fund Christopher Columbus' voyage to America. In Britain Saxons, Danes and then Norman Kings pawned all they could to fund their war efforts.

What we think of as modern pawnbroking, however, was 'invented' by the Medici banking family from northern Italy in the middle ages and when they split up the family between the bankers and the pawnbrokers, they also split up the family crest, with the pawnbrokers taking the 3 balls sign.

But pawnbrokers have never had an easy run, there has always been a social stigma to overcome. Richard 1st had a special pawnbroker tax; Edward I, whose money management was extremely poor, found a unique way of avoiding redemption costs, he banned all Jews (who made up most of the pawnbrokers at the time), from the kingdom for the next 300 years, but it didn't stop Edward III pledging 5 of his crowns, and 2 Earls, whom he sent to Belgium to be locked up as collateral, and hence the term pawn was applied to the game of Chess.

The Catholic Church succeeded in banning money lending across most of medieval Europe, and it recovered only to be lampooned as Shylock in Shakespeare, the dirge of the working classes by Dickens in A Christmas Carol, and by Nazis who blamed money lenders for profiteering.

Nevertheless pawnbroking has always survived, with ups and downs such as the doldrums with the post war advent of social welfare. So why does it always bounce back? The answer is that there is always a market and a need for alternative credit. Not everyone has a bank account, in Britain 8 million people don't. Since the March 2016 budget 9 UK banks are legally required to offer very basic accounts to these people, but this will not help those people achieve loans or overdrafts. As we shall see later, Credit cards are also increasingly restricted, but the reality is that as long as you have an item to pawn you can get a relatively cheap, fairly instant loan without the need for further credit checks since the loan is secured against property just like say a re-mortgaging contract. Looking at this from another angle you could say that right now in the UK , every bank is effectively pawnbroking but just under another name – they are securing loans from creditors such as central banks by pledging their assets (unencumbered assets- in the jargon). Mervyn King the former Governor of the Bank Of England went as far as to say in February 2016 that Banks should behave more like Pawnbrokers and the world would be a better place for it. Pawnbroking has always oiled the wheels of commerce whether for King, country, small and large businesses, or for individuals needing short term loans.

It is important to differentiate pawnbroking from PayDay unsecured loans which have been rightly criticised for their high interest rates. In the case of Pawnbroking those who borrow against assets have no problem with the product, 88% in research by the National Pawnbrokers Association state they are completely happy with the service [1], it is those who never use a pawnbroker and wouldn't know where to even find one who seem to profess to judge those who do.

There is nothing new in the world of loans; Richard I set about regulating pawnbrokers just as the FCA do now, and the 14th Century Catholic Church set about a campaign to remove money lenders from the High St. much as Ed Milibands Labour manifesto recommends.

Meanwhile Kerry Catona has taken out loans, Paul Weller and Bradley Wiggins have posed outside a pawnshop, and Eric Clapton is quoted as always looking in pawnshop whilst on tour seeking out interesting guitars.

This book takes a look at how pawnbroking has changed over the years from a service for Kings down to social help for the poor and everyone in between. It charts the changing face of pawnbroking and how it fills a social need right now, and how it is fast becoming the

---

[1] Bristol University Research 2011

loan of choice for small and medium sized businesses and increasingly the middle classes. It concludes with a look to the future.

Chapter 2 What is Pawnbroking and how does it work?

> Most people think there is a stigma around Pawnbroking and that the pawnbroker is out to catch you.
>
> This is not correct. If you can't repay the loan after the term, you can repay the interest and start a new loan or you can just let to be sold. In most cases the profit on the sale comes back to the customer anyway. It's a quick and easy process which is simply misunderstood by most people.

You may believe there is a stigma around pawnbroking and that it would be justified. If that is the case I would ask you to suspend your disbelief that it could be otherwise whilst you learn a little more about how it works and how it fits into society. Subsequent Chapters will of course explore pawnbroking down the ages and particularly focus on the Victorians and the 20th Century right up to modern day pawnbroking. But first of all it's important to understand what Pawnbroking is and how it works right now.

So we will start with a little background. The sector is called the 'alternative credit lending market' and is rarely out the news at present whether it's a fly on the wall documentary like 'Pawn Stars', a story within a soap opera like 'Coronation Street' or a Hollywood blockbuster. Politicians and the media are quick to slam the outliers in the alternative credit markets and those who charge extreme interest rates.

But who or what is a pawnbroker? At a simple level a Pawnbroker is;

> "a person or dealer licensed to lend short term money at a specified rate of interest on the security of personal property, which can be sold if the loan is not repaid within a specified period in order to recover the debt".

Clearly in a modern context there are precise meanings attributed to the exact process of pawnbroking and the compliance with rules that govern them, which in the UK are part of the Consumer Credit Act 1974 and across Europe the EU Consumer Credit Directive 2010, but as a working definition the one above works well enough.

To put more flesh on the bone, the word *pawn* is derived from the Latin *pignus* meaning 'pledge' and is effectively a form of secured short-term lending which is nowdays defined in law as a period of 6 or sometimes 7 months, as opposed to a mortgage with is a secured loan lasting perhaps 25 years. Compared to unsecured loans such as so called Pay Day loans they are inevitably much cheaper because the pawnbroker does not have to factor in the risk of the customer not returning. In the terminology a 'pledge' is the transaction involving handing over 'pawn' to the broker whereby the customer pledges to return within typically 6 months to 'redeem' the item by paying the loan back plus the agreed interest.

This is how it works in diagrammatical form;

To expand on this the process is as follows;

1 The Pawnbroker estimates value of the item and says what he is prepared to lend and the interest rate

Like banks, a pawnbroker earns interest that is charged on the loan of a pledged item. In order to accept goods into pawn, a pawnbroker makes an on-the-spot valuation of the goods. The customer and the pawnbroker will agree the sum to be lent and the pawnbroker and the customer completes a loan application process. Customers can borrow as little as £5, and all they need to do is bring in the item, proof of identity and/or proof of address. This could be a recent bill, driving license and so on. The pawnbroker will value your item and decide what they can lend you, typically up to 60% of the second hand saleable value.

2 Customer agrees to loan and reads the paperwork

At the point the customer's details are completed, they receive a document called a 'Pre Contract Information' (SECCI or Standard European Consumer Credit Information) which highlights the key points of the agreement including the interest rate and the APR (annual percentage rate). The agreement is in a standard format as decreed by the EU, so that loans from different providers can easily be compared. It allows the customer to confirm that they are happy to accept the terms of the loan. The customer will then need to decide whether to go ahead with the transaction then signs the actual agreement with details of his rights and protection under the Consumer Credit Law and the terms and conditions of the loan. The customer also receives as part of the document a pawn-receipt for presentation when redeeming the goods. The document gives full details of the withdrawal notice, and customers are verbally told this and their other rights at the point of sale. The credit agreement is also known as the 'pawn receipt'.

3 Customer given the pawn receipt, valuables put in safe

The customer signs to say they wish to proceed and the pawnbroker will log a copy of the 'ticket' with the item and put the item in the safe, or secure it elsewhere if it's a larger item. The customer immediately receives their money. The agreement is usually, and as a minimum always, for a period of six months. A customer has the right to give notice to withdraw from the agreement within 14 days and also has a right throughout the lifetime of the agreement to make partial or full early repayments.

4 The loan can be redeemed any day and interest paid up to that day

They are entitled to redeem property by payment of the original loan plus the interest amount due at any time during the contract period. When the loan and the interest are paid, the goods are immediately returned to the customer. If the customer has not repaid the loan during this time and the loan was over £100 he will receive notice that the property is due to be sold and giving him a further statutory period of 14 days in which to redeem, the customer will normally however have the option at the end of the contract to renew the loan. If they do not redeem the property by the end of the contract, and if the loan received was more than £75 the pawnbroker will sell the item, notify the customer of the sale within 20 days and after deducting what he is owed, return any surplus funds back to the customer.

5 If not redeemed profit on sale is generally returned to the customer. The vast majority are redeemed

Only when the loan was for less than £75 will the unredeemed property become the pawnbrokers to do as he wishes with. However, most pawns are redeemed within time, and to back this up Bristol University Research in 2010 suggested that around 88% of goods are redeemed. In those cases of non-redemption whereby the customer does not renew or respond to the notice served, the pawnbroker may take steps to dispose of the goods. Having served the notice of his intention to sell the goods the pawnbroker is obliged in law to obtain the 'true market value' of the goods on the date of sale. This ensures a true price is obtained for the customer for their goods. Where the proceeds of sale are greater than the amount due to the pawnbroker, the balance is due back to the customer. If there is a shortfall, the pawnbroker cannot legally chase the customer for further debt unless he has carried out a full creditworthiness check on the customer, which a pawnbroker will rarely do. The whole point of a secured pawn loan is that a full credit check is not required since the security is the asset. The worst that can happen is that the customer loses the item. They will not be chased for any further debt, they will not have debt collectors or bailiffs knocking on the door, or face a mountain of spiralling debt under ANY circumstances.

The Pawnbrokers Perspective

Against popular belief, the pawnbroker does not wish to gain title to property as he is in the business of lending money and he wishes far more to see the loan repaid without needing to resort to the sale of property. This way not only is the debt cleared in full, but the customer is happy at the return of his goods and he has possession of them to return again at some stage in the future if he ever needs to borrow again. This is proved by the very high levels of redemption of pledged goods and by the volume of trade that is repeat transactions - nearly always with the same security time and again – a bit like using the pawnbroker as a local ATM machine!

Some pawnbrokers will increase the pawn period to 7 months specifically so that they don't end up owning title to an item pawned for less than £75. This is not entirely out of altruism, as nice as some pawnbrokers may be. They don't wish to have to get embroiled in VAT documentation. So long as they don't own title there is legally no VAT to pay.

So the pawnbroker is generally a professional tradesman who wants to keep his database of customers, build relationships and customer trust. He does not want to own title to the goods, and most definitely does not want to receive stolen goods not least because it there were a police seizure they would be unlikely to get much compensation for being the victim of crime themselves.

Pawnbrokers used to be thought of in the dowdy dusty image inspired by the Dickens story or perhaps the 'Pawnbroker' silent movie featuring Charlie Chaplin, but if you were to walk into a pawnbroker's shop today you could be forgiven for thinking that you had just walked into your local bank or building society. Pawnbroking in the jargon can now be seen as a 'serious alternative' to using the services provided by the High Street bank. It appears that customers have realised that borrowing money against goods they already own is an affordable alternative to a bank overdraft or other type of loan. Indeed the research by Bristol University [2] confirmed that those who regularly used a pawnbroker were generally happy with the service under the circumstances- that is to say nobody really wants to have to borrow money or pay interest;

> "The vast majority of customers we surveyed (95 per cent) were satisfied with the service they received from the pawnbroker they used. Eight in ten customers would use the same company again. Customer service, the speed of the loan decision and convenient location were the things that customers expressed most satisfaction about" Personal Finance Research Centre, Bristol University

---

[2] Bristol University Research 2011 'Pawnbroking'

The big disappointment for these brokers today is that still only 3% of the adult population use pawnbroking as a form of financing. Pawnbroking businesses are everywhere on the High Street if you know where to look for them. They are often also jewellery retailers, giving them a perfect shop set-up for lending and for keeping jewellery goods safely in storage. Consequently, the security that the vast majority of pawnbrokers give loans against is gold, jewellery and watches. This is because they are easy to store and value, do not perish or generally depreciate, and have an immediate second hand value.

Case Study

One property developer managed to halt a repossession order by pawning his Bentley GT. He found himself in an unfortunate position just as he was nearing completion on a property development, the banks called in his loan. He was able to borrow 50k from Prestige Pawnbrokers in Surrey, which enabled him to market his property and sell in his own time, thus averting financial disaster and ruin.

Recently Prestige Asset Finance was visited by a wealthy woman who was in the middle of a painful divorce. Without available cash to pay her children's school fees, she was able to offer her Patek Philippe watch and her engagement ring as well as the logbook against her Range Rover to enable her to borrow 30k to keep the wolves from the door whilst waiting for the divorce settlement to be decided.

Whilst pawnbroking offers a better rate than a typical unsecured loan, the point the Government and media often make is that people need to be aware that any form of borrowing- secured or unsecured can lead to spiralling debt. Like any business relationship it is a matter of how much risk the broker is prepared to take and how much trust he has in the person's ability to pay back. Pawnbrokers are legally acting as a 'bailee for reward' and as such the pawnbroker has a duty of care to his clients and their property and must replace lost or damaged items with equivalent value and there are plenty of laws enforcing this and defending the customer.

The APR Calculation

One issue which complicates the process and muddies the water in most people's minds is the impact of the Consumer Credit Directive 2010 from the EU parliament. This decrees the usage of APR calculations- the Average Percentage of Repayment. The logic for the APR is that if everyone expresses a loan as though it were for one year, the customer would be able to choose from a level playing field. So for example 6% per month over 6 months would have an APR of 84.9%. Pawn loans are really designed for short term borrowing but the APR calculation gives a method by which borrowers can compare cost between lenders at least to some extent. The typical pawnbroking loan is redeemed after about 3 – 4 months and so most are redeemed early. Many are repaid within thirty days and so for example after one month the customer would typically repay £6 in

interest and the £100 loan, totalling £106. So the confusion amongst customers is as follows. If I borrow £100 at 6 pc for 6 months this would have an APR of 84.9% and yet I may know that I intend to repay it at the end of month one. I would therefore have paid 6%

interest, so how useful was the knowledge that the APR was nearly 85% in a year if I never intended to have a loan for a year?

Here is an example of the full calculation and you will be pleased to know there won't be a test afterwards and I am showing it simply to make a point about its complexity. Assume that the transaction is for a loan of £100 at a monthly rate of 7% i.e. £7.00 per month on a 6 months contract, i.e. it is a single repayment contract with all amounts due repayable as a single lump sum at the end of the contract on redemption. Let us use the actual number of days of the loan rather than months and for this example take the start date as 1st January 2013 with termination date 30th June 2013.

$$\text{APR (\%)} = 100 \left\{ (1 + C/P)^{y/t} - 1 \right\}$$

C = Interest = 42.00 (6 months at £7.00 per month)
P = loan = 100.00
t = 181 days out of 365 (6 months)
$$\begin{aligned}
\text{APR(\%)} &= 100\,[\,(\,1 + 42/100\,)^{365/181} - 1\,] \\
&= 100\,[\,(\,1.42\,)^{365/181} - 1\,] \\
&= 100\,[\,(\,2.02815\,) - 1\,] \\
&= 100\,[1.02815] \\
&= \mathbf{102.815}
\end{aligned}$$
Giving us an APR of 102.8%

The purpose of showing this is just to demonstrate just how impractical it is for the regulators to assume that this calculation makes life more transparent for the average customer. Even worse politicians, media and governments constantly misinterpret and misunderstand these figures, and is it any wonder?   In short they quote annualised compound rates for financial products designed in some cases for loans for just a few weeks and wonder why it is a large number when compared to something designed for 25 years which is factored down to just one year for comparison purposes.

We could agree that an APR is a useful tool and of course is *the* recognised mathematical calculation for comparing lending products, but in reality it is not always quite so great at making a comparison between a long and short-term loan product.

Here is the great irony. The EU introduced APR calculations to achieve transparency for EU customers. Before 2010 and the Brussels calculation, the calculation for pawnbrokers went like this- If you borrowed £100 at 6% you would pay back £106 if you redeemed anytime during month one, or £112 during month two and so on. Everybody understood this and barely a calculator was needed. Since 2010 the above formulae is applied and the exact charge per day is calculated, and if you redeem early, the law states that because the contract is broken the pawnbroker is due compensation of up to 28 days interest. So now if you come in early during the month to redeem you might pay say £4 interest but if you come in towards the end of the month it may be £8, but if you wait until the end of the month it will be £6. The APRs quoted and the actuarial daily calculations have caused such confusion that many pawnbrokers have waived their entitlement and settled for the £6 rather than charge the extra for early redemption in this example.

Many economists have also questioned the use of APRs in demonstrating the cost of short term loans which were never intended to be taken out for a year because it is an annual measure. It therefore makes longer term loans look cheaper and short term loans look more expensive by multiplying them by a factor. They would say it is not a good measure because it compares secured loans designed for the short term with products like mortgages which are a

commitment for up to 25 years. If a friend lent you £20 on Friday and you paid him back on Saturday and bought him a half pint of beer to thank him, the APR of that transaction would be close to infinity and yet to most people that would sound perfectly reasonable.

Here are some similar examples to explain this.

1 You go for a weekend away with the girls, but forget your purse. A friend lends you £50 for the weekend, and you repay her with a glass of wine the following week. You have just paid a % APR which is close to infinity in effect, but are you furious? No, you are delighted she was able to help you out.

2) You travel to London to see its wonderful parks or galleries, and at the posh hotel reception are told it will be £100 per night. Do you jump up and down and say "Hey, that's £36,500 a year just for one room !!!" or do you happily sign in, delighted that there is something so clever as a place where you can go for instant accommodation when YOU need it.

3) Sometimes you travel by train, and travel hundreds of miles for relatively little money per mile. However, trains cannot come to your door at 1:00am and take you directly to the party to collect your stranded teenage child! A taxi will be more expensive per mile, but for the shorter, bespoke journey and immediate availability you are again delighted that the option is available.

The point is that the cost of a product is not always price – in real life you have to pay for speed and convenience and immediate accessibility.

The Parliamentary Select Committee on Pay Day Lending 5th November 2013 heard evidence from the trade, other stakeholders, the FCA, OFT and Government minister Jo Swinson and most of those interviewed said they though using APRs for short loans was a poor measure and a much better measure would be the absolute cost in money terms. In other words if I borrow £100, how much would I actually pay back at the end of the term?

Research I undertook for the National Pawnbrokers Association (June 2013) suggests that whilst 98% of the public have heard of pawnbroking, only 3% have ever used a pawnbroker. The majority actually have no idea how it works but interestingly once it is explained to them around 30% would definitely be interested in the future of considering pawnbroking. No-one understood how APRs worked or how to interpret them properly.

Interestingly in parliamentary debate in June 2013, MPs asked why rates were so confusing and shouldn't they be made much simpler whereby you were just quoted the cost in money not APRs? The irony being that that is exactly how life was before 2010 when the same parliament changed how pawnbrokers made the calculations to make the process more transparent. Politics has a short memory perhaps.

Despite this relatively small market place, there is certainly no shortage of interest in becoming a pawnbroker. The NPA receive around 60 requests for application forms from would be pawnbrokers per month and in 2013 around 5 a month succeed in fulfilling legal and other requirements and become members. This has recently declined rapidly because of problems for pawnbrokers opening bank accounts, a theme we shall return to in later chapters.

So who are the customers?

The 3% of the population who use pawnbrokers are typically regular repeat users of pawnbroking. Many return and redeem the same pledges over and over again, I heard one lady in a shop in Eltham, Kent call her pawn ring her lucky ring and kiss it before handing it back to the shopkeeper.

> Elaine Jones, 57, is in and out of Pawnbrokers every few days. Today she is here about a gold bracelet. "I pawned it a year ago and I've come to pay it over, I can't really afford to get it out…it was a way to get the money rather than a Pay Day loan which charges a lot more
>
> April 2013

There is certainly a sense of security from an item that you know you can use as security if you need to. Customers can come from all walks of life and borrow money for all sorts of reasons. The main drivers for a customer using a pawnbroker are speed and convenience and the main reason is to pay utility bills or seasonal needs such as Christmas presents or birthdays. For the Asian community gold bangles and other such wedding items may be taken out from the pawnbrokers for the wedding season and then returned to pay for other pressing needs. Most customers are borrowing to satisfy short-term cash flow needs – and especially since the 2007 credit crunch all sections of society tend to be affected by cashflow problems at various times in the month or year. Larger cash loans against luxury items that customers can do without for a period of time are increasingly common. The growth in the market in 2012 was 15% driven by loans to small businesses who found themselves unable to obtain bank loans to bridge cashflow needs and high net worth individuals pawning an exotic range of items such as classic cars, designer handbags, property and fine arts and jewellery.

Purpose of Loans (BIS June 2013)

	Pawnbroking Loan
Day to Day expenditure	36%
Special occasion	21%
Energy Bills	11%
Other	32%

'my husband and I had emptied our savings in order to raise the 25 per cent deposit we needed to buy our house three years ago,' says Kate, who lives near Harrogate, North Yorkshire, with Chris, an IT manager. 'So in March, I pawned my Mulberry Bayswater handbag that cost £800 and a Gucci bag made from python skin that cost £2,000. That gave us the £1,000 we needed to cover our winter utility bill.

Here are more examples from 2013 quoting a pawnbroker and then a customer;

"We've loaned against everything from boats, planes and helicopters to a Picasso and a Lowry," James Constantinou, Prestige Pawnbroking.

"You just can't get a bank loan for a couple of months, we just don't have that relationship with them anymore." Mark Landsberg-handing over keys to his Porsche 911 to pay a tax bill

CASE STUDIES

1. A local restaurant recently pawned their fine wines to raise cash to help them back on their feet after several bad months of business due to people dining in rather than out.

2. A City banker who had been made redundant loaned against his black Lamborghini for four months until he found new employment.

3. A pawnbroker helped one family prevent a repossession of their home by lending money against a 20k diamond ring of 4 karats. The family were able to pay the four months arrears, avoiding an eviction and giving the borrower time to market the property and set up a manageable repayment scheme until the property sold.

Another pawnbroker AT Pledge in Northampton have also loaned against private planes and even hired an aircraft hangar to store them. Recently a retired FTSE director started a pawnbroking business exclusively dealing in classic cars. Apart from being a keen collector himself his logic was that country houses are expensive to maintain and who would notice if one of a number of hobby cars disappeared for 6 months?

A key factor in most transactions is the speed aspect. Since items are secured against the loan there is no need for credit checks and long loan application processes. In addition, small businesses increasingly look to bridge cashflow shortages caused by, for example, debtors, tax demands, rent, payroll or business development. Online pawnbroking companies have also emerged and have seen growth through giving greater flexibility in the variety of pledges they may take and store.

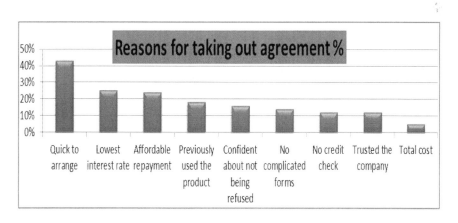

Bristol University Personal Finance Research Centre report - Pawnbroking Customers in 2011

Pawnbroking is a positive growth story due to the lack of available bank credit. A pawnbroking loan is a short term loan secured against something of value that you own. It is therefore, completely different from unsecured borrowing such as payday loans or doorstop lending, which can balloon. Pawnbroking is essentially nothing other than a low value mortgage, and generally cheaper than an overdraft, which is why there is still scope for more pawnbrokers and certainly more customers.

Ian Williams was the first online pawnbroker to offer loans against designer clothes and accessories (pawnbrokeronline.co.uk). 'Often women find that their wardrobes rival their jewellery boxes when it comes to their most valuable assets,' he says. 'One client needed urgent dental work so borrowed £1,500 against five pairs of Chanel shoes, all of them boxed with their original receipts and in pristine condition.

Pawnbroking customers pledge property and consider the loan as simply turning their goods temporarily back into cash as they once were. In other words customers feel they are simply, in effect, borrowing from themselves. No fuss, no favours, no extending or creating unsecured credit with the threat of negative credit ratings or 'blacklisting' as it is known if the loan is not repaid. Fully secured, straightforward and transparent credit in minutes at a reasonable cost – these are the attributes that people value from pawnbroking.

When her husband, Jon gave Jessica Humphreys a £12,000 black Hermes tote bag two years ago, she thought she would never let it out of her sight.

'It was a present for my birthday and I treasured it, keeping it in its luxurious soft dust bag and bringing it out on special occasions only,' the interior designer recalls.

'Then, last month, we were hit with a few big bills — £6,000 for our kids' school fees and £1,500 for some emergency rewiring — which we couldn't afford. That's when I thought the unthinkable and sacrificed the Hermes.'

Financial expert Jasmine Birtles, of moneymagpie.com, urges caution. 'On the whole pawnbroking is much better than some other forms of borrowing, like a payday loan,' she says. 'But people should always shop around, getting their item valued by several pawnbrokers and checking the interest rates and loan periods. If you're attached to an item, think carefully about pawning it and how certain you are you'll be able to repay the loan in six months' time.'

Could I be a Pawnbroker?

Finally in this Chapter we should look at the market and how a new **pawnbroker would go about starting up. The Pawnbroking market in the** UK is currently growing at 15% a year but compared to the consumer credit market it is a relative minnow at less than £1 billion. There are over 2000 stores employing over 10,000 staff. Loans are typically repaid within 4 months and the average loan is rising towards £200. The average customers is likely to be female and is most likely to be pawning a ring. Most customers redeem and will return, showing loyalty to their pawnbroker. The key data for 2012 from the NPA is shown below. Apart from the credit crunch growth has been fuelled by the increase in gold price. The value of gold has increased tenfold since 2002 until June 2013 when the price dropped by 20%. The increase in value has meant that the value of items people wish to pawn has typically risen so they have been able to borrow more.

2013 Pawnbroking Market

Pawnbroking market	£850m
Average Market Growth	15%
Direct employment in Pawnbroking	10,000+
Pawnbrokers stores	2000+
Average loan	£150 to £200 - 2 to 3 times a year
Loans per year	Over 2 million
Average time to repay	3.5months
Redeem within 14 days	Circa 10%
Sex of customer	Female 59%
Redemption rate	88% redeem
Customer satisfaction	95%
Customers loyal to one Pawnboker	71%
Complaints to Ombudsman Upheld in 2012	2
Most popular item pawned	Gold ring
Number of UK adults that don't have a bank account	8 million+

Anyone thinking of establishing a pawnbroking business will need to satisfy a number of criteria in addition to possessing the fundamental ability to run a new business. Firstly they will need access to at least £100k and a current bank account, a Consumer Credit License which is issued since 2014 by the Financial Conduct Authority(FCA). They will require modern pawnbroking software in order to join the NPA, good quality security and eurograde safes to store the pledges, and of course insurance. Cashflow is King, a pawnbroker who runs out of lending money is dead in the water of course.

An understanding of the evaluation of jewellery is also key, if you can't value the items how can you risk lending against them? And finally an understanding of the law is necessary- The Consumer Credit Act 1974 sections 114 to 122 of the Act and particularly of these following Regulations made under it, most notably the Consumer Credit Directive 2010 which has specific rules around advertising and promotion as well as how APRs must be calculated and displayed.

It may be worth the start up pains because the market is one of the few success stories since the credit crunch of 2007.

Other International Markets

The international arena has developed in a similar way with more or less restrictive practice depending on the regime. In the United States each state makes its own rules as part of the federal system. Pawnbrokers are generally issued licenses under the authority of the Mayor, or in some cases like Massachusetts, by the Boston police department. In the state of New York permits are renewable annually on payment of a fee, and the pawnbroker must file a surety bond with the Department of Consumer Affairs, for the sum of $10,000. The business is conducted on much the same lines as the UK but the rate of interest is typically slightly less. Loans tend to be written for a period of 4 months, with an additional 30 day grace period and rarely for over 6 months.

Unredeemed pledges may be sold at any time after the legal time for the loan. New York contains one pawnshop to every 12,000 inhabitants. On this basis pro rata there should be twice as many pawnshops in the UK, in other words there may be scope for around 5000 stores. In the state of Massachusetts unredeemed pledges may be sold four months after the contract date. The licensing authority may fix the rate of interest, which may vary for different amounts, and in Boston every pawnbroker is bound to furnish to the police a daily a list of the pledges taken in during the preceding twenty-four hours, specifying the hour of each transaction and the amount lent if asked to do so.

In modern Europe the fact that many pawnbrokers are either a state or a municipal monopoly necessarily places them upon an entirely different footing from the British pawnshop. Unlike the UK Government most pawnbroking countries do not apply the Consumer Credit Directive 2010 for pawnbrokers and the rules are less demanding .

Obviously rates vary but a French loan would typically be between 7% and 12% per month. The profits are paid over to the Assistance Publique, the comprehensive term used by France authorities to indicate the body of charitable foundations. There are around sixty pawnbrokers in Paris alone but their level of business is relatively small compared to the UK. The amount that can be advanced by a municipal pawnshop is fixed by an official called the commissaire-priseur. They will lend up to 80% against precious metals and 66% from other items. Loans are granted for six months but were traditionally for twelve months, with the right of renewal. Unredeemed pledges may then be sold by auction, but the proceeds may be claimed by the borrower at any time within three years. Pledge debts can be paid off by instalments. Around fifty French towns possess municipal pawnshops, and a few of which charge no interest at all.

Pawnbroking in Germany is conducted both by the state, cities and by private business all competing with each other. For state controlled shops the maximum and minimum rates of interest are fixed, but the rate varies in much the same way as the UK Post Office offers rates for savers in an open market. 80% of wholesale value is advanced on silver, and 83% on gold. Loans run for six months, but a further six months' grace is allowed for redemption before the article pledged can be sold by auction. The net annual profit usually amounts to little more than I % upon the capital employed.

In Italy, the country of origin of the mont de piété, the institution still flourishes. Four-fifths of the value is lent upon gold, silver and jewels, and two-thirds upon other articles. Monthly interest is typically between 5 to 7%. A loan runs for six months, and may be renewed for similar periods up to a maximum of five years. If the renewal does not take place within a fortnight of the expiration of the ticket, the pledge is sold, any surplus there may be is repaid to the customer. The amount to be advanced by a municipal pawnshop is fixed by an official and the borrower has to pay an agents fee of 2%, which is deducted from the loan. Private pawnshops also exist in Italy, under license from the police, but they charge very high interest.

The monts de piété in Spain charges typically 6% upon advances which run for periods varying from four to twelve months, according to the nature of the article pledged, and a further months grace is allowed before the pledges are sold by auction. Private pawnbrokers are also very numerous, but charge about 60% per annum. They are popular because they will allow much larger advances. Finally across the border, the system in Portugal is very similar to the UK with no restrictions and limits.

So in conclusion to this section it's interesting that although there are common elements to pawnbroking around the world each country has introduced its own nuances and interpretations. General rules have been introduced in Europe and the UK is one of the few countries to not opt out its pawnbroking community. Whether this is good or bad for the customer is a moot point, however, what it does mean is that in complying with laws around APR calculation it is much harder for the UK customer to understand the real cost of the loan because of the APRs. The old English phrase they 'can't see the wood for all the trees' springs to mind.

I hope this chapter has dispelled the myth of the money grabbing outlaw that has been depicted in folklore of the trade of pawnbroker. The process is , for better or worse, thoroughly regulated and those you are practitioners in the trade are in the most part fair honest and decent people who make a living but do not rip-off their customers or extort their position. The 3% of the population who use pawnbrokers regularly and the new entrants from business and the traditional middle classes are often done a huge disservice by the 97% who know nothing about the service but profess to express a view on the topic, some vocally. We shall see in subsequent chapters that it was ever thus.

Chapter 3- Pawnbroking Down the Ages

'...it is a dirty-looking, dusty shop, the door of which stands always doubtfully, a little way open: half inviting, half repelling the hesitating visitor. The pawnbroker himself .. treats his customers with the greatest lack of consideration and courtesy, the new customer looks cautiously around to ascertain that no one watches him, and hastily slinks in...... A few old china cups: some modern vases, adorned with paltry paintings....several sets of chessmen, flutes, fiddles, prayer books and testaments. Two rows of silver watches, numerous table and tea spoons, cards of rings and brooches, cheap pans and snuff boxes, five or six beds, strings of blankets and sheets, silk and cotton handkerchiefs, wearing apparel, planes, chisels,saws, which have been pledged and never redeemed.......

Charles Dickens

If your view of pawnbrokers is similar to that of Mr Dickens[3] then read on and see if your view changes when you have more context to consider his opinions.

---

3   C. Dickens, *Sketches by Boz*, 1836, Scenes - Chapter 23

Having been introduced to current processes and how they work you will be wondering where did it all start?....It's true to say that most people think they know what Pawnbroking is and how it works, but they are usually wrong. As Kenneth Hudson correctly asserts [4] , for

such an important aspect of history, society and business you would be hard pressed to find much written material on the people who use pawnbrokers, and even more pressed to find anything that has been written that is either positive or at the very least neutral. The famous historian G.M. Trevelyan [5] 's 'English Social History; a Survey of Six Centuries, Chaucer to Queen Victoria' goes out of its way to not mention pawnbroking or any other type of lending at all. Major thinkers throughout history—Plato, Aristotle, Thomas Aquinas, Adam Smith, Karl Marx, and John Maynard Keynes, to name just a few, considered moneylending, at least under certain conditions, to be a major vice without particularly exploring the theme. Other writers from Dante, Dostoyevsky, Shakespeare to Dickens have generally had a negative view of the profession. In Arthur Conan Doyle's 'Adventure of the Red Headed League', a London pawnbroker is duped into a scam whilst his shop is robbed.

---

[4] 'Pawnbroking- An Aspect of Social History' Kenneth Hudson 0 370 30447 0
   Bodley Head, London, 1983.

[5] 'English Social History; a Survey of Six Centuries, Chaucer to Queen Victoria' G M Trevelyan published in 1942

With that exception where the pawnbroker is merely gullible, they are most often portrayed as the bad guy. Perhaps the most famous is Goldfinger from Ian Fleming's James Bond series, who is a corrupt pawnbroker set on world domination. So how did it all start and why did it get such a bad press?

Origins of Pawnbroking

Most people are in fact surprised to learn that pawnbroking originated at least 3,000 years ago in China, where borrowers could take up to 3 years to repay their debt with an interest rate cap of 3% per annum. We could go further and say it is one of the oldest professions and certainly pre-dates banking. An old joke has it that prostitution is the oldest profession, jewellery manufacture is the second oldest so the client can pay her, and pawnbroking is the third oldest so that she can pawn it when times are tough. Nobody would believe this to be true but the fundamental point is that there are always people who have money to lend and other people who want to borrow it, and bringing the two together, when done in a professional manner, is beneficial to both sides. It makes it possible for people to spread payments, make investments and order their lives in a way that is convenient to them. At the same time it makes a profit for the person on the other side of the transaction who has excess capital to lend out. This is what the Victorians would have called 'oiling the wheels' of commerce.

Origins Of Pawnbroking

1000bc China- Pawnbroking to advance Empire

India- common barter

Ancient Greeks- international trade

Roman Empire-trade

The focus of pawning in imperial China, however, was very different though, it was typically to fund wars, for ship-building or for business enterprise. As a pawnbroker you would probably be lending to Kings and mandarins of the society- high net worth customers. The idea spread to India and Europe and loans were typically required by the rich for the same reason and by Kings and dynasties to defend their realms and for waging wars for which mercenaries and barons needed payment. For the greater part of history it is the rich who have engaged in pledging not the poor as Dickens would have us understand.

The interesting point about China is that having led the ancient world in enlightened lending, for most of the last century pawnbroking was banned in China under Chairman Mao. It is only in recent years that it has taken off again. The re-invented pawnbroking community is a little different now though. I spoke in June 2012 to leading company the Bailian Group, Vice President Zhou Jidong who told me that in modern Shanghai they have 2 sides to their business; the consumer pawn stores are inside Department Stores and the typical transaction is £350, whereas their business-to-business pawn is typically for pawning sheet metal for ship building with a typical pawn being £150,000. The shipbuilders pawn the raw material and draw it off when they have the contract to build in place. The current problem for China is that the laws and principles for pawning are antiquated so they were visiting England to understand how EU law worked and whether something similar would work in China. It is ironic that the country that probably invented pawnbroking is now looking to the west to understand it better.

The ancient world may not have recognised the term Pawnbroking, but they would certainly have recognised the process as a form of secured usury. This was known to both the Ancient Greeks and Romans, and the original Roman Laws form the basis of most of the laws we have today. The Greeks used brokering as a means of affording imported grain and in return exported their ideas philosophy and know-how across the ancient world.

Elsewhere in the ancient world brokering was nevertheless also alive and well. The Hittites, the Egyptians and the Phoenicians were all lending each other food, substances, other bits and pieces and getting them back, this is the ancient history of usury or pawnbroking, and it is clearly part of human nature to lend things and have them returned at interest.

In the wake of the Romans in Britain Saxons, Danes and then Norman Kings pawned all they could to fund their war efforts and consolidate power, and in Europe we can similarly thank the pawnbroker indirectly for the discovery of the Americas. As we noted before, Christopher Columbus' voyage was funded largely by the proceeds from pawning Queen Isabella of Spain's jewels.

So the process of Pawnbroking was all set up , what could possibly go wrong? Oh yes, 1500 years of religious doctrine.

The Influence of Religion in Society

Pawnbroking and moneylending has always had a difficult relationship with religion and most have at some time tried to ban moneylending. However the need for money for investment and managing finance is so fundamental to human life that it is impossible to stop as religious leaders , politicians and intellectuals have found down the ages. Laws and decrees that would aim to abolish lending only serve to push the profession underground.

It all started to go wrong with the ancient Greek intellectuals. The practice of lending money at interest was met with hostility by Plato and his young student Aristotle (384–322 b.c.) who believed the practice to be unnatural and unjust. In the first book he wrote:

> "The most hated sort is usury, which makes a gain out of money itself, and not from the natural use of it. For money

was intended to be used in exchange, but not to increase at interest. Of all ways of making money this is the most unnatural. "

Aristotle believed that charging interest was immoral because money is not productive. If you allow someone to use your orchard, he argued, the orchard would bear fruit and therefore is productive, but he considered money to be purely a medium of exchange. Money does not create more money it is just barren. £100 pounds now is the same as £100 any other time. In the modern world we would frog march the young Aristotle straight down to the London School of Economics or Harvard and enrol him straight on a course, but it goes to show that even the great minds of the ancient world could not get their collective heads around the concepts of investments, interest and economic stimulation.

In ancient Rome 'money begetting money' was found everywhere. The Romans were quite restrictive however, in terms of what could and couldn't be pawned. You could not pawn for example, clothing, furniture, or tools of your trade. The emperor Augustus converted the surplus from property confiscated from criminals into a special fund from which sums were lent to those who had assets worth twice the pledge value- a sort of early lottery scheme you might say. But Roman usury also had its critics. Seneca at the time of Christ certainly agreed with Aristotle and said so in no uncertain terms, Cato the Elder had previously famously compared usury to murder and Cicero wrote that "these profits are despicable which incur the hatred of men, such as those of lenders of money on usury."

This all led to a much bigger issue for money lenders which made the Romans look like mere grumblers, and that was the attitude of religion and various religious leaders to the business. Unfortunately, most religions tend to say something on the topic. Usury is an issue that has troubled theologians over the years. The Old Testament includes particularly strong statements against it for example Exodus 22:25:

"If thou lend money to any of My people, even to the poor with thee, thou shalt not be to him as a creditor; neither shall ye lay upon him interest."

Even in the Book of Exodus, limits are being set on the amount that may be charged on the repayment that is to come. In the book of Deuteronomy it says;

'No man shall take the nether or the upper millstone to pledge, for he hath taketh a man's life to pledge'

Or in modern language don't pawn the tools of your trade or anything you need in order to survive, which seems rather obvious.

<u>Religion Against the Pawnbrokers</u>

Jewish-   Okay to lend but only to non-jews
Christian- No moneylenders near the temples please
325ad-   Nicaea- Priests banned from being Pawnbrokers
768ad-   Charlemagne banned Money Lending by Christians
Muslim-   Outright ban on 'interest' although to sell and buy back later at a
higher price is okay
1139   Lateran Council in Rome introduced restricted licences
1175   10th Sitting of Lateran Council-pawnbroking briefly legal
1274   Council of Lyon-illegal again
1311   Council at Vienna- Stop press- Usury is sinful

The councils of the Church have variously considered the matter. On both scriptural and moral grounds, Christianity opposed usury from the beginning. The early church saw itself as having the God given right to take the high ground or any ground they so wished on any issue which they considered had a moral element, which meant pretty much everything. It was a strong Christian King who made a stand for instance against a papal decree because there was strong belief that it came from God and you could find yourself in the fires of hell for all eternity for disobeying the word of God.

And the Church began to throw it's weight around by decreeing various restrictions. The Council of Nicaea banned the practice among clerics and decreed that those who were allowed to take up the profession could only charge 1% per month, which made it a completely unviable business proposition, there was literally no interest in this. Under Charlemagne, the Church extended the prohibition to laymen. By the 12th Century, the second Lateran

Council in Rome had denounced usury as a form of theft, and required restitution from those who practiced it and the Council of Vienna declared that any person who dared claim that there was no sin in the practice of usury be punished as a heretic.

There was, however, a loophole in nearly all of these pronouncements: the Bible's double standard on usury. The Bible permits Jews to lend to non-Jews. This reading had positive consequences. For lengthy periods during the Dark and Middle Ages, both Church and civil authorities allowed Jews to practice usury. Kings and barons requiring substantial loans in order to pay bills and wage wars, happily allowed Jewish brokers into their states. Thus, European Jews, who had been barred from most professions and from ownership of land, found moneylending to be a profitable, albeit hazardous, profession.

It was not a happy relationship though. The bible had virtually carved out a monopoly for the Jewish lenders. Although Jews were legally permitted to lend to Christians, and although Christians saw some practical need to borrow from them and chose to do so, Christians resented this relationship. Jews made profit from an activity that no-one else was allowed to do for fear of eternal damnation.

Opposition to Jewish usurers was generally destructive. At the end of the 12th Century, the Jews of York were massacred in an attack planned by members of the nobility who owed money to the Jews and sought to absolve the debt by removing the pawnbroker through violence. During this and many other attacks on Jewish communities, accounting records were destroyed and Jews were murdered. A good reference on persecution of the Jews can be found in Simon Schama's works[6]

One side beneficiary of this persecution was Oxford University. Whilst Jews were prevented from taking part in many trades since they were unable to swear a Christian oath, they were allowed to work at the University as doctors, landlords, pawnbrokers and teachers of Hebrew.

From the Christian perspective, the theologians had a huge problem. Why did God allow Jews to lend to non Jews but a Christian couldn't lend to anyone? Unfortunately St. Jerome (347–420) came up with an answer. He stated that it was wrong to lend to your brother, which he interpreted as other Christians, however it was fine to charge interest to one's enemy. Usury was perceived as a weapon that weakened the borrower and strengthened the lender, therefore, if somebody lends to their enemy that's okay because ultimately they would suffer. This created the bizarre situation that Christian brokers would not lend money to Crusaders who went to fight the Holy Wars, but would lend money to their enemies the Saracens who were fighting back against the Christians.

---

[6] The Story of the Jews, Simon Schama 2013, and the BBC Production 'Story of the Jews Sept 2014

Apart from the illogical absurdity of helping your enemy on the basis that at some point in the future they may live, or die, to regret it, perhaps the biggest injustice to economic development indoctrinated in religion was the concept that there always has to be a winner and a loser. So if the lender was the winner the borrower must be the loser. The concept of 'win-win' was yet to be invented. The dark and middle ages were the era of the zero-sum game- someone wins someone loses but the pot stays the same size.

My favourite quote however comes from a bishop called Jacques de Vitry in 1214;

> "God created three types of men: peasants and other labourers to assure the subsistence of the others, knights to defend them, and clerics to govern them. But the devil created a fourth group, the usurers. They do not participate in men's labours, and they will not be punished with men, but with the demons. For the amount of money they receive from usury corresponds to the amount of wood sent to Hell to burn them."

One could have observed that the priests didn't exactly get their hands dirty in the way that the poor peasants had to either, why were the clerics placed in a position where they merely govern, lucky old them?

Other writers of the day were equally damning against usury. The Italian poet Dante (1265–1321) very kindly placed usurers in the seventh rung of Hell in his 'Inferno', with heavy bags of money tied around their necks for eternity.

> "From each neck there hung an enormous purse, each marked with its own beast and its own colours like a coat of arms. On these their streaming eyes appeared to feast."

Profits, so said Dante, should derive from the fruits of labour—and money lending entailed no actual work. He believed that the deliberate act of lending money was the worst sin imaginable. He debatably didn't have very much imagination.

The trouble with the middle ages, or perhaps more likely the middle aged theologians, was that they probably had too much time to think. The more they thought about interest on loans the more abstract the conclusions. A popular view typified by the 12th-century English theologian Thomas of Chobham was that lenders were effectively making a profit on 'time' based on the fact that all they were actually adding to the deal was time. And yet 'time' belonged to God, so these lenders were making profit from something they did not own, and even worse, had actually stolen this 'time' from God. Luckily for the money lenders God never bothered to raise a charge of profit by fraud or extortion in the civil courts.

More cynically clerics from the 1100s onwards frequently manipulated and selectively enforced the usury laws to bolster the financial power of the Church. When it decided to keep its own borrowing cost low, the Church enforced the usury prohibition to cap rates. At other times, the Church itself readily loaned money for interest. Monks were in reality among the earliest moneylenders, offering carefully disguised interest-bearing loans throughout the Middle Ages, but of course the money was to forward Gods work so that was okay.

One way around the doctrine came about in the 13th Century when a theologian invented the concept of 'interest'. The word comes from the Latin verb 'intereo', which means "to be lost." Interest was considered compensation for a loss that a creditor had incurred through lending. Compensation for a loan was illegal if it were a profit, but if it was merely reimbursement for a loss or an expense it was acceptable. Interest was therefore a matter of "damages repayment" . Therefore, interest was sometimes allowed, but always frowned upon. It might seem a matter of semantics but to the pawnbroker and often his customers, it was success versus starvation.

To the Muslim sharia law to this day, making interest on a loan is unacceptable, but one way around this is to agree a price at one point and a price to buy it back later so that it is a buying and selling contract and not technically a matter of interest. This form still exists today and is called a 'Sale and Buy Back' contract. This is typically more expensive than pawnbroking and offers the customer none of the protections of the Consumer Credit Act, which we will discuss in future chapters. Even the Jewish Mosiac Law, the law of Moses, forbade charging interest to poor people, however, they could lend to gentiles and take interest, which is another good reason money lending originally focused on the rich, or at least the 'not poor' and of course the non-jewish, who were considered fair game.

The early Christian Church dealt with the problem of usury by regarding any economic motives with great suspicion and felt that the urge to make money, like other passions, needed to be kept under tight control. Trade could only be carried out for the public good- 'pro bono publica'. But ironically the Church administrators found they could not avoid pawnbroking and usury activity because at the heart of the church was a complex administration and the machine only functioned by allowing IOUs, loans and pawns. In fact the Catholic hierarchy frequently allowed usury when money was lent by their important friends, such as Florentine bankers, whilst demonising Jewish and other ethnic moneylenders. These merchants are seen historically perhaps like modern bankers were seen prior to 2007, as conservative figures who knew the money markets and gave back generously to fund the arts and support good works as philanthropists, and nowadays the modern equivalent being sponsoring a premier league football team. Contrast this with the image of the jews as money grabbing usurers. Both were effectively involved in pawnbroking but one lent to the Church and high society and the other to the down and outs of Florence. Generally when the economy was doing well, the Church and other leaders looked the other way and saw money lenders as crucial to society but in depressions they were easy scapegoats.

If I were a typical pawnbroker in Europe in the first millennium A.D. I would be jewish, living in a capital city near the King and nobility. I wouldn't lend to other jews, or to most people in fact because they would have little wealth to pawn. Possibly I would consider a small loan to a skilled artisan who had tools of his trade but it would be unlikely. Most customers would be well to do, rich and need money for a project such as a new building. I would typically earn a few per cent per month and be repaid in a year's time. I may have to move to another area or kingdom if the going gets tough. There is a risk I could be outlawed at any time and bad debts are possible. I would be hated by the church and many others, unless of course they needed a loan.

negative right up to the 19th century, but in some parts of Europe the churches view was being weakened. The Reformation across northern Europe brought acceptance of usury. Martin Luther in the early sixteenth century, believed that commerce and the Church were completely different spheres, one being Gods realm and the other being man's. He could see no reason why the church should interfere with man's commercial activity. He didn't like moneylenders any more than the Catholic Church but in a sense had the view of a mother seeing her boys come back from school with muddy trousers after a game of football, in other words 'boys will be boys' or in this case 'men will be men'. Men were too corrupt to not want to engage in business.

It would be easy, however, to be lulled into a false sense of security here though. Luther was definitely not a fan and wasn't planning to pawn his watch anytime soon;

> Earth has no greater enemy of man, after the Devil, than a gripe-money and usurer, for he wants to be God over all men. Since we break on the wheel and behead highwaymen, murderers, and housebreakers, how much more ought we to hunt down, curse, and behead all usurers.

The more enlightened views came from John Calvin, (1509–1564), a theologian who thought that moneylending was fine as long as it was fair and reasonable and was broadly in line with Christians values. So , for example, the pawnbroker should establish that the person was wealthy enough to repay the debt, and that if someone was struggling to pay Christian principles of charity and support should be applied.

I can't help but think that if the Church had applied a lighter touch and not simply interpreted their beliefs in a way that saw them dominating commercial decisions and business, pawnbrokers could have been more accepted and a better integrated part of society. It cannot be a positive aspect of economic development to have religious decisions dominating commerce.

This conflict between religious belief and money lending came into focus again in July 2013 when the Archbishop of Canterbury, Justin Welby, vowed to put payday lenders (short term high cost credit lenders of unsecured loans) out of business by using the Church to build up Britain's network of credit unions. He told Errol Damelin, the founder and chief executive of Wonga (the largest unsecured lending corporation), about his ambition to make the controversial lenders redundant – by helping the 500 financial co-operatives, which already provide small loans to their members, play a much bigger role in helping people with money problems. The Church of England he stated had already set up a credit union for its own staff and would allow them to use its buildings and schools and encourage Church members with the right expertise to volunteer with them. The church he said has 16,000 branches in 9,000 communities – more than the banks. In an interview with Total Politics magazine, he said: "I've met the head of Wonga and we had a very good conversation and I said to him quite bluntly 'we're not in the business of trying to legislate you out of existence, we're trying to compete you out of existence.'

"We're putting our money where our mouth is, we're starting a Church of England staff credit union. You've got to have a corporate interest body to identify who's members of the credit union. We're starting one of those so we're actually getting involved ourselves. We're working steadily with the main trade bodies for the credit unions."

Wonga insisted that it would welcome competition from credit unions. Mr Damelin said: "The Archbishop is clearly an exceptional individual and someone who understands the power of innovation.

We discussed the future of banking and financial services, as well as our emerging digital society. There is mutual respect, some differing opinions and a meeting of minds on many big issues. On the competition point, we always welcome fresh approaches that give people a fuller set of alternatives to solve their financial challenges. I'm all for better consumer choice."

The outcome was that by the end of 2013 Wonga's business had increased significantly off the back of the publicity and the Church scheme has possible run into opposition from within its ranks such that nothing has happened yet at the time of writing. I wrote to the Archbishop and asked if I could join the committee reviewing this. I had pointed out that the rate the church considered aspirational was actually higher than a pawnbroker charges and therefore he had no need to set up new stores in churches because my members would do it for him and cheaper. I received a polite but firm decline to my offer.

Credit unions set up by the UK Government by the Department for Business Innovation and Skills plans to provide £35m over 10 years to help credit unions grow which is very little, so interference by church and state in the commercial market mechanism has not proved very successful in this millennium….. or the previous two.

Intellectual Views

The Church were not alone in their negative stance to pawnbrokers, and it may be no co-incidence that the Church was very influential in education over the last 2,000 years. But Aristotle has no logical reason for his anti-business world view.

Intellectuals Against Pawnbrokers;
Aristotle- Money adds no value to life people shouldn't profit from it.
Cato the Elder- usury is just like murder
St Jerome- it's OK to lend to your enemy so that they suffer
J de Vitry- Money lenders will burn in hell fire
Dante- the 7th rung of hell's ladder is reserved for them
Thomas of Chobham- they have stolen 'time' from God
Pope Sixtus IV- detestable to God and man.
Shakespeare- moneylenders are like Shylock
Henry Fielding- they grow fat by sucking the customers blood
Sir Walter Scott- second class citizens
Martin Luther- After the devil they are biggest enemy of man
Dickens- ultimate depravity- like Scrooge
Karl Marx- enemy of the people
Dostoyevsky- murdering a money lender is more palatable than other murders
Arthur Conan Doyle- they exist for the gullable
Beatrice Potter- The most [dockers] can do…in their helplessness is to make pawnbrokers their banker and the publican their friend (from 'Life of East London')

---

reserved for what would happen to you in the afterlife not in this life, the non-Christian or the non-believer had a definite advantage in plying their trade since it did not occur to the Church hierarchy that they could possibly be wrong about the afterlife. And what an amazing weapon of war ! Arm your enemy with superior weapons bought from you by pawns so that they can defeat you in battle but with the certain knowledge that one day they would go to hell for taking a pawn loan. Meanwhile in the short term I wonder if any of the crusader peasants had time to reflect on the fact whilst being bludgeoned to death by an enemy with superior weapons, that the last laugh was on the enemy...... come armageddon.

The Second Milennium Pawnshop

By the second millennium the pledge system had developed in Italy alongside accounting and Pacioli's double entry book keeping and ultimately the Lombardian banking system which is the basis for banking and alternative credit as we know it today. The pledge system which became almost universal on the continent of Europe arose from the 11th Century. Its origin was purely benevolent, through the early 'monti di pieta' in Italy and 'monts de piete' in France , which were sort of pledge taking charity shops. These charity shops were established by the authority of the Pope to lend money to the destitute without charging interest, so long as the loan was covered by the value of the pledges. In other words a bit like going into a charity shop today with an old book and being given £1 for it so long as the volunteer shop assistant thought you looked poor enough.

Inevitably because they relied entirely on monks and others giving time free they ultimately failed. A similar experiment was undertaken in Freising, in Germany, and in Salins, Franche-Comte, however by then interest of 7.5% per annum was charged which was still extremely cheap.

The Vatican reluctantly sanctioned the *Sacri monti di pietà* which were shops officially able to charge enough interest to make a satisfactory profit. However, not for the first time, this led to huge controversy within the Church based again on the Christian concept that you should not charge interest. For years the controversy rumbled on until Pope Leo X in the tenth sitting of the Council of the Lateran of 1175 declared the pawnshop was a lawful and valuable institution, and threatened anyone who thought otherwise with excommunication. This ultimately led to St Charles Borromeo establishing state owned pawnshops. The decree was overturned in 1274 at the Council of Lyon. All in all being a pawnbroker was a challenging occupation for some 600 years. The issue as you will have realised was about the extent the church should get involved in managing and running pawnshops rather than let the evil money lenders make the profit.

The Italian pawnshops became common place in most Italian towns by the 1400's, and all of them made a profit. The first records of pawnshops are from 1464, when the earliest accounts are of a store in Orvieto personally opened by pope Pius II, possibly in the way a celebrity would cut the ribbon on a new supermarket nowadays. Shortly afterwards another was opened in Perugia by 2 Fransican monks called Barnabus Interamnensis and Fortunatus de Copolis, who have the distinction of being the world's first known and named Pawnbrokers. They collected funding for initial capital by street preaching, and made a substantial profit in their first year of trading.

This idea was copied by other Fransiscans, and Pope Sixtus IV in Savona. To slightly digress- what an incredible name Sixtus Four (IV) is, almost an oxymoron. There was also a Sixtus Five but there has never been a Sixtus Six. It was originally planned that the new Pope in 2013 would be adopting this name but he chose not to- what a shame.

Even though he supported the idea of helping the poor in principle, Sixtus V proclaimed that charging interest was;

> "detestable to God and man, damned by the sacred canons and contrary to Christian charity."

So pawnbroking has caused a problematic issue for hundreds and thousands of years and has been debated by theologians, politicians and economists almost since time began. It certainly had an image problem and really needed a medieval PR guru to sort itself out.

One man who was perhaps worthy of such a title was Father Bernandino di Feltre, who was ultimately canonised and opened stores in Assisi, Mantua, Parma, Lucca, Piacenza. Padua, Vicenza, Pavia and many other places. So Pawnbroking was alive, well established in middle ages Italy and even had their own saint.

The Dominicans who were more puritan in belief, much like Oliver Cromwell's Roundheads, fought tooth and nail to stop the Fransicans setting up their stores, however, the largest objectors were the Jews in

Florence who no doubt felt the monks rates were too cheap and therefore unfair competition to them. Ironically it was a Dominican who set up the very first Florentine pawnshop, but he needed to get the local priest to declare charging interest was not a sin to keep the authorities happy with this, and presumably to save his own soul. Even more ironically what with the Pope granting licenses all over Italy for pawnshops, it wasn't until some 70 years later in 1539 that the first pawnshop opened in Rome. From Italy the concept of the pawnshop spread gradually all over Europe. Augsburg, Nurnberg and then Amsterdam, Brussels, Antwerp, Ghent and Madrid where a priest opened a charitable pawnshop allegedly with the princely sum of five pence taken from a charity box.

If I were a typical pawnbroker between the 12th and 18th Century I would be in competition with the Churches charity pawnshops. However I would charge slightly more, perhaps 7% a month but would be in a position to lend a more meaningful amount of money which would attract much more business. My customers are typically of a lower social order since the rich prefer to deal with the Lombardy banking community. I may have a shop but equally I may have traded in the tavern.

Inevitably it wasn't long before the rich merchants started to get involved in the profession, which became the beginnings of the business-to business lending market, or in other words merchant banking. The industry as we know it today can be traced back to fifteenth century Italy when the noble Medici family was a dominant financial power. When the family was split in two, one half of the family became bankers and the other, pawnbrokers. The latter took with them the family crest, which incorporated the now instantly recognisable sign of the pawnbroker, the famous three gold balls. It should come as no surprise that the origins of banking and pawn lending are so closely entwined – taking a pawn is, after all, in the words of the Office of Fair Trading in 2010, 'simply another form of banking'.

This was a pivotal moment in medieval Europe. Apart from giving us the brand of the 3 balls, the Medici family gave pawnbroking a sense of respect that had been lacking Roman times. Here was a serious family business of bankers becoming involved in developing pawn loans as a business proposition. In many ways this then started to ebb away at the power of interference previously expressed by the Church. It was hard for the Vatican to complain too much whilst they also borrowed from the same family from time to time.

The Customer is 'the' King

In England the pawnbroker literally came in with William the Conqueror. He brought financiers as part of his entourage to accumulate, valuate and if necessary pawn jewellery and treasure that he 'accumulated' en route. We can perhaps imagine a production line of plunder- pillage- pawn. It was by now commonplace for Kings to accumulate a good deal of jeweller mainly because of its easy to pawn qualities rather than any desire to collect treasure per se. The early Popes used to sleep next to a large hole full of treasure to make sure nobody stole it whilst they were asleep, perhaps we can imagine early Popes like Smaug in JRR Tolkiens 'The Hobbit' sitting on top of a pile of treasure.

Kings Against Pawnbrokers

William I- cruelty
Richard I- imposed taxes
Edward I- banned for 300 years
Henry V-refused to pay back debts
Henry VIII- banned moneylending (unsuccessfully)
James I- passed Act against corrupt brokers

By all accounts these early pawnbrokers to the rich and famous were treated with cruelty. Most of these money men or usurers were either Jews or Lombardy merchant bankers. The former were not treated well. A good example of how they were treated can be found in the character of Isaac of York in Sir Walter Scott's 'Ivanhoe'. Isaac was considered a second class citizen to be lampooned and derided and not quite human.

So pawnbrokers have never had an easy run, there has always been a social stigma to overcome. Richard 1st had a special pawnbroker tax, he needed the money for crusades but realised by imposing a tax he could effectively give himself a reduction in repayment; Edward I, the incorrigible spendthrift, having racked up a stupendous bill for pawns to build Castles and support his army of barons and merchants, found a unique way of avoiding redemption costs, he banned all Jews, who made up most of the pawnbrokers at the time, from the English kingdom for the next 300 years, and most decamped to Brussels. He was able to do this because of the Papal decree outlawing usury and more significantly because the Italian Lombards were building a firm foundation for commercial lending. Part of the dislike of the money lenders may stem from the rates of interest charged, according to Roger Creet[7] interest varied from 43pc to 65% (time period not clear). Samuel Walter Levine[8] in Hume's 'History of England states Henry III, in 1272 decreed that Jews were to be restricted to interest of 45pc. Or 2pc a week for the poor scholars of Oxford.

• The treatment of the Jews of Oxford is of particular historical interest. They first came to England with William the Conqueror and were welcomed in Oxford from 1080 to 1290.Unlike other areas, the Jewish lenders here suffered no persecution, in fact they received royal protection, with Kings of England taking a personal cut from their profits. In return they were protected by the king's Constable of the Castle. This lasted until Richard I needed money for crusades and later to pay his ransom after being taken prisoner.

---

[7] Pawnbroking And The Working Class1850-1941 R Creet 2013
[8] A Treatise On The Law of Pawnbroking   Samuel Walter Levine

His brother John, levied massive taxes on the lenders. The significance of the Jews being in Oxford was in supporting students and academics needing money for their studies and accommodation to rent. The Jewish community became embedded and provided teachers and professors, doctors, landlords, as well as pawnbrokers and money lenders.t riots when books remained in Jewish hands. After Edward I banned all forms of usary they mostly left for France with everything they could carry.

So pawnbroking continued as usual for the rich. In fact Edward III pledged 5 of his crowns, and even 2 Earls from Derby and Northampton, whom he sent to Belgium to be locked up as collateral. In fact this human pawn may be the derivation of the term 'pawn' in the game of chess, with the pawn being peasantry who were generally considered expendable and tradable in exchange for a nobleman. It was not uncommon to pawn your Bishops and Castles as well. In the example of Edward however, things did not end happily. His failure to redeem made two leading Belgian Finance Houses bankrupt, and it is not clear what happened to the pawns, the poor old incarcerated Earls. Another example would be Henry V who did much the same, getting heavily into debt and then refusing to pay back the broker.

But it wasn't just Kings behaving badly, so too were the other nobility. The most outrageous debtor ever to set foot in a pawnbrokers was Guy, Count of Flanders who in 1278 owed 6,800 lire, which is equivalent to a pawn of £10 million today. It is not clear if he was ever able to repay the debt but it's unlikely because he died a pauper. Another tactic was used by Charles the Bold, Duke of Normandy in 1473. When no pawnbroker would give him a loan he revoked all licenses and only gave them back to those who agreed to lend to him. It took 45 pawn shops to satisfy his ambitions.

The Pawnbroker in Society

For the Jewish businessman the second millenium was a difficult time. They were banned by the Church from taking jobs in guilds or handicrafts and the list of things they couldn't do meant that money lending was one of the few professions they were actually allowed to do. Ironically, the Church came out against moneylending at various times in the dark and middle ages as we have seen earlier in this chapter, mainly because it wanted to save the souls of Christians and felt that moneylenders would surely go to hell. However since they felt that Jews were almost certainly going to hell anyway the fact that they were pawnbrokers didn't really matter so much since the Church believed their souls were already lost. Having been banned from most tradesmans' jobs including making jewellery, money lending was something they were effectively forced into even though their capital was eroded by mob attacks and the occasional massacre. In the later middle ages Jews tended to lend to the poor and Lombardians to the rich.

Throughout history there has been two tracks of pawnbroking, the commercial and sometimes dangerous business of lending to Kings for profit, and attempts typically by religious factions to provide social support to the poor, which was generally in competition to the Jews who charged more. In England in 1361 Michael de Northborough, bishop of London bequeathed 1000 silver marks for the establishment of a free pawnshop. Like its Italian , German and French predecessors it also failed. Europe wasn't ready for social pawnbroking, a kind of Oxfam meets soup kitchen.

After the fall of Richard III, the Lombards' built a stronger base in England.

This negative views of lenders was reflected in much of the writing of the day. Characters in plays popped up with names such as, my favourite, Sir Giles Overreach, Mr Lucre, and Mr Bloodhound. And of course 'The Merchant of Venice' by William Shakespeare (1564– 1616), with the rich , in every sense, character of Shylock. Here a poor nobleman, if that is not a contradiction in terms, called Bassanio, establishes a loan from Shylock. The pawn in this case is a pound of flesh from his friend Antonio. Knowing Bassanio's credit record Antonio must have either liked him very much or been keen to lose some weight. Sisson[9] argues that Shakespeare however, would have known and used the lenders of London and their reputation was generally positive, so in placing Shylock in Venice he is likely

---

[9] A Colony Of Jews In Shakespear's London   by Charles J Sisson 1937

differentiating between the Lombardy based Jews and the London Jews.

But it wasn't only Jews lending money, the City Guilds did so as well. The Drapers Company and Merchant Taylors' Company delivered pledges, often for liverymen to buy property. Church wardens acted as pawnbrokers for parishioners needing money to hire tools of their trade such as cows and shears. According to Addy[10] by 1590 the rate was 5pc per month.

One spectacularly ambitious plan came from the courtiers of his son Charles I at the time of the English Civil War. The idea was to make Charles I a pawnbroker with £100,000 capital to be raised by the City of London and the King personally benefiting to the tune of 66% of all profit. Thereby the King would be helping the poor get slightly cheaper loans than usual and if there had been a Guinness Book of Records at the time they would certainly have got in it with the longest title for a proposed Bill

"The intolerable injuries done to the poore subjects by brokers and usurers that take 30, 40, 50, 60, and more in the hundredth, may be remedied and redressed, the poor thereby greatly relieved and eased, and His Majestie much benefited". The reform of "brokering pawn" was much discussed but no action ever taken.

---

[10] Church and Manor by Sidney Oldall Addy

Whilst the King failed to become a celebrity pawnbroker, interestingly, the Bank of England under its charter, does have the power to establish pawnshops. It was the original intention of it's first directors to offer the poor a secured lending service that charged 1% per month interest. Again this never happened, who wants to be responsible for setting up a business for such a low return.

Across the whole of Europe including Britain, the 16th century brought about a renaissance, and all the great explorers were eager to establish trade routes to the New World and Asia. Unprecedented trade meant unprecedented investment. It signalled the greater acceptance of interest for both pawnbrokers and the banking system. In the same way as London currently positions itself as a global centre for finance and premier stock exchange, at this time the merchants of Genoa, Venice and Florence had a relaxed attitude in order to attract business to their cities.

The Netherlands and Belgium benefitted from being a corporate centre for the Lombard money lenders in the middle ages. Interest rates were heavily controlled there, as long ago as the 17th century the Archdukes Albert and Isabella, reduced the annual rate of interest from 32.75% to 21.75% and mont de piete stores flourished. Similar stores to this were introduced in Spain by Ferdinand of Bavaria. He ordained that the net profits were to accumulate, and the interest upon the fund to be used to reduce the charges. The original rate was 15% per annum, when the Lombard money-lenders had been charging 43%. Not surprisingly the shops were so successful that for many years their rate of interest did not exceed 5% pa. finally increasing until 1788 and even then only by 2.5%. So perhaps you can give money away after all.

The working capital of these official pawnshops was provided by charitable institutions or the municipalities. The rate of interest charged in various parts of Belgium and the Netherlands varies from 4 to 16% so it paid to shop around. Unredeemed pledges were sold publicly 15 months after being pawned. As in the rest of Europe the most popular pawns were and still are jewellery, gold and diamonds.

Broking was on something of a roll now, especially in northern Europe, but the pawnbrokers shop as we know it hadn't fully developed. There were many places you might go to get a loan. For the ordinary person in the 17th and 18th Centuries the place you would most likely go to in order to pawn your goods would be the public house. A great example of a pawnbroking pub still standing is the Castle pub in Farringdon ,London. It was frequented by King George IV, who enjoyed cockfighting. Arriving without money, he issued the pub with a pawnbroker's licence and instantly became the first customer by handing over his gold watch so that he could gamble with the loan. Both pawnbroking in pubs and cockfighting were subsequently stopped by Act of Parliament so you won't find either pursuit in this pub today, however the bear is very good.

Interest in Pawnbroking was also developing in France. Whilst it was equally controversial in medieval times, it ultimately became legal when Jean Boucher published his *Défense des monts de piété* in 1695. The first monte de piete in Paris did not open until 80 years later by royal patent. The statistics which have been preserved relative to the business done in the first few years of its existence show that in the twelve years between this time and the Revolution, the average value of the pledges was 42 francs. The interest charged was 10% per annum, and large profits were made. Commercial pawnbrokers were briefly allowed to co-exist until in 1806 Napolean Bonaparte re-established the monopoly of state pawnshops. The pledge shop became in effect a department of the administration.

The view of the pawn shop as a den of inequity became more prevalent in Britain. The origin of this negativity most likely stems from the actions of the Charitable Corporation who effectively became the first ever large scale pawnbroker, lending to struggling businesses and the poor. The company published its business model in 1719, setting out its practice. The procedure was that a borrower took goods to one of the corporation's warehouses and signed a bill of sale, or contract, The warehouse keeper valued the pledge and he and an assistant signed a certificate. This was passed to the book-keeper for entering in the corporation's accounts, and then to the cashier who paid the borrower his loan. Both the warehouse keeper and the cashier were required to give security, and there were surveyors of warehouses to act as a check on the warehouse keepers. Furthermore the books were signed every night. Unredeemed pledges could be sold after a year.

Whilst this was a great idea, the management turned out to be highly corrupt, dealt in stolen goods, speculated recklessly, and aided and abetted defrauding of creditors. As a result the business collapsed spectacularly. The profession recovered only to be lampooned as the dirge of the working classes by Dickens in his work 'The Pawnbrokers Shop' [11]1835 he describes it as follows;

---

[11] The Pawnbrokers Shop Charles Dickens 1834

" Of all the numerous receptacles for misery and distress with which the streets of London unhappily abound there are perhaps none which present such striking scenes of vice and poverty as the pawnbrokers shop. ...It is a low, dirty-looking, dusty shop, the door of which stands always doubtfully, a little way open: half inviting, half repelling the hesitating visitor." This was how Charles Dickens depicted a pawnbroker's shop in Drury Lane circa 1835. The customers include a prostitute and a man with an 'inflamed countenance and drunken stagger', an 'ill tempered brute who beats and kicks his wife' and who is 'in the last stages of consumption'. The pawnbroker himself is an 'elegantly attired individual with curly black hair, diamond ring and double silver watch-guard, who treats his customers with the greatest lack of consideration and courtesy', and finally a new customer 'looks cautiously around to ascertain that no one watches him, and hastily slinks in'. This is a theme developed in Pickwick Papers his first novel. Not surprisingly Pawnbrokers today are not best pleased with the legacy view of pawnbrokers even though the profession has changed beyond recognition. One chain of pawnbrokers in modern day south London call themselves with tongue in cheek 'Pickwick Pawnbrokers'.

But it was not all totally one sided. A more positive view was taken by Jeremy Bentham (1748–1832) the philosopher who published a thought paper called *'A Defense of Usury'* [12] Bentham argued that any restrictions on interest rates and any other kind of limitations of

---

[12] In Defence of Usury, J Bentham

lenders to ply their trade were economically harmful because they restricted an entrepreneurs ability to raise funds. It is obvious to us and indeed was obvious to him that if you were to invest in something inherently more risky you would expect a better return on your investment. Since new ventures involved high risk, they could only be funded at high interest rates. Limits on permissible interest rates, he argued, would kill innovation, the engine of growth. The same argument incidentally, was put forward by the UK Government in 2013 when challenged to cap interest rates for Pay Day lenders.

Correcting another common error, Bentham[13] also maintained that restricting borrowing forced borrowers to go to illegal lenders who would charge them more. Again this is an issue in modern times, the argument goes- if legislators make it so unfavourable to lenders that lending money isn't profitable, the legal lenders won't bother lending whereas those outside the law, the 'illegal loan sharks' in modern parlance, will still carry on outside the law but will put their interest rates up because their legitimate competition has evaporated. You should also know two other things about Jeremy Bentham- his major contribution was his advocacy of contractual freedom- the greatest wealth and happiness for the greatest number, and secondly that you can still see him today. When he died he was stuffed and mounted in a cabinet in the entrance to University College London except for his head which is kept in the chancellors safe.

---

[13] A Defence Of Usury, Jeremy Bentham 1787

Bentham's contemporary the economist Adam Smith (1723–1790), ultimately believed the state should set interest rates but nevertheless wrote the simplest and most compelling defence of moneylending: "As something can everywhere be made by the use of money, something ought everywhere to be paid for the use of it."

You may have been mistaken for thinking that surely Karl Marx, the free thinker who gave us the fundamental communist ideology would be in favour of pawnbroking and other money lenders? Not a bit of it, he chose to copy all the deep prejudices from the Church of the middle ages, and even in the anti-establishment Dostoyevsky's *Crime and Punishment*, the disgusting old lady whom Raskalnikov murders is a usurer. Which it would seem makes the murder more palatable to its Russian audience.

Pawn shops continued to grow in number up to the first world war. In Britain in the latter stages of the nineteenth century and early twentieth century there were nearly as many pawnbrokers as public houses. However, between the wars the post great war generation were less inclined to use money lenders because of the return to near full employment as the economy grew and with the growth of social security and increased prosperity in the sixties pawnbroking hit an all-time low.

With the influx of the Welfare State, social benefit and the health service, and the fact that pawnbroking was still linked to an archaic act from a century before, the post Second World War welfare reforms nearly finished off pawnbroking and meanwhile in Germany

Chapter 4- Pawnbroking Law Development

Pawnbroking is now highly regulated by government through the Financial Conduct Authority, but there have always been rules and regulations of some kind and a procession of laws over the last millennia. This chapter looks in more detail at the laws affecting pawnbrokers down the ages.

We have seen that in the period before the sixteenth century whether forms of usary were welcomed or banned depended on whether the King needed money for wars and whether they were prepared to pay the interest on the loan. By the 1500s the rules were relatively simple. You needed a local license as an official broker from the town authority or mayor. To get a license you had to be of good standing and keep records of all transactions.

The separation from Rome made the profession more acceptable because the Roman Catholic Church had always had a difficult relationship with the concept of interest.

1571 Legal rate set at 10pc maximum

In 1571 a legal rate of maximum 10pc was passed despite effectively 25 years of opposition from the Church.

1603 Pawnbrokers Act

This was the first ordinance specifically passed by parliament and was targeted at the fraudulent and criminal brokers masquerading as authorised traders. A clause also officially authorised the owners of stolen goods to demand the immediate return of those goods based on showing evidence of ownership. The Act specifically stated that this was not intended to be harmful to Pawnbrokers of good repute;

"…..but rather applies to persons…..who gave up their manual occupations and set up a trade of….taking pawne, finding that their riseth and growth to them a more readie, more profitable, and speedier advantage and gaine then by their..manuall labours….."[14]

1623 Maximum Interest Reduced

Maximum interest was reduced from 10% to 8%

1638 City of London Pawnbrokers Register

Charles I wanted a register of Pawnbrokers. There was clearly a desire to stop unscrupulous lenders at the time and Creet[15] points out citing an anonymous writer in 1678;

---

[14] Law of Pawnbroking   Levine
[15] Pawnbroking ad The Working Class Roger Creet 2013

"An unconscionable Pawnbroker…lives and grows fat on Fraud and Oppression….He is Treasurer of the Thieves Exchequer, the common fender of…Shoplifts in the Town. To this purpose he keeps a private warehouse and ships away ill-gotten Goods by Wholesale"

1694 Bank of England

In its first manifestation the new Bank Of England was set up and functioned as a pawnbroker. They gave 4pc loans against non precious metals as a 'lombard' for lending money on small loans. Lombard St exists to this day in the City of London. This seems to have been an unsuccessful venture.

1745 Petition of Pawnbrokers

This is the first known collective action or lobbying by the larger pawnbrokers on becoming sickened by the constant bad image of their 'brand'. Their recommendation was for the trade to be licensed nationally and the interest raised to 20%, of which 4% would go to good causes like hospitals and warehouses. This is also the first example of a call for a sort of lottery tax and was clearly aimed at improving the image of the pawnbroker as a philanthropist. A parliamentary committee was set up to hear the issue and a

pawnbroker called Richard Grainger[16] stated that he lent on over 24,000 pledges a year for an average 15p each (3 shillings) and these were typically for small businesses. It was stated that the average profit of a pawnbroker was around 16pc a year, a good but not exceptional return.

Although the Committee Stage went well the following year a bill was passed that would have imposed an outright ban on pawnbroking. This would have been catastrophic for the country as there were over 250 pawnbroking shops in London alone, so there was clearly a need for the service.

1751 Tippling Act

This was good news for pawnbrokers because it clamped down on the illegal pawnbrokers. One sector in particular had always frustrated the pawnbrokers and this was the licensed trade. Publicans had long since excepted pawns over the beer counter, and it was thought by many pawnbrokers to be here that many of the stolen goods would be fenced.

1752 Interest Rate Amended

Interest was reduced to 6pc on a loan

1756 Pawnbrokers Act- Usury Law amendment

This was good news for pawnbrokers because it exempted pawns of less than 10 pounds (most of them) from Usury Law.

---

[16] House of Commons Journals Volume 25 1745

1784 Pawnbroking Act

This act bore the snappy sub title;

> 'Bill against divers persons of ill fame and repute, who live in garrets, cellars and other obscure places, taking upon themselves the name of Pawnbroker'.

It came about because there was concern by parliamentarians about unscrupulous pawnbrokers who were accused of charging 2.5% a week interest APR over 150%, substituting goods with inferior product and selling pledges within 3 months.

This established a maximum interest rate for loans over £10 (£1,000 today based on average earning power) at 15% a year. This clearly did not affect most pawnbrokers who were trading loans at well below £10. More significantly the Act also required pawnbrokers to register as pawnbrokers, which was the first occasion on which such a register was used as a form of license to trade. The maximum loan period was set at one year although six months was the norm.

1800 Pawnbrokering Act

This was the most significant act so far and fell in George III's reign. It was the blueprint for modern laws. The driver of the Bill was a Lord Eldon who made no secret of the fact that when a young barrister he was much indebted and valued the support of his local pawnshop. The pawnbrokers were grateful, and for many years after Lord Eldon's death they continued to drink his health at their trade dinners. The measure increased the rate of interest to 20% a year. Loans were to be granted for a year, but pledges might be redeemed up to fifteen months, with one week to be interest free. The Act also interestingly established a reward for 'common informers' who reported illegal practices by pawnbrokers.

The National Pawnbrokers Association have an original bound copy of the Act. Complete with original handwritten notations from the Pawnbrokers Society from 1921.

Pawn Brokers Society 1831

ANNO TRICESIMO NONO & QUADRAGESIMO

GEORGII III. REGIS.

****

C A P.   XCIX.

An Act for better regulating the Business of Pawnbroking.   [28th *July* 1800.]

WHEREAS an Act was passed in the Thirty-sixth Year of the
Reign of His present Majesty, intituled *An Act for regulating* 36 G. 3.
the Trade or Business of Pawnbrokers, which was to be in recited.
force for Three whole Years, and from thence until the End of
the then next Session of Parliament, and no longer: And whereas it
is expedient that Provision should be made for more effectually regulating the Trade or Business of Pawnbrokers, from the Time when
the said Act will expire: May it therefore please Your Majesty that it
may be enacted; and be it enacted by the King's most Excellent Majesty, by and with the Advice and Consent of the Lords Spiritual and
Temporal, and Commons, in this present Parliament assembled, and by
the Authority of the same, That the said Act, passed in the Thirty-sixth
Year of the Reign of His present Majesty, for regulating the Trade or
Business of Pawnbrokers, shall be and the same is hereby declared to be
in full Force and Effect until the Expiration of the present Session of
Parliament, and from and after such Expiration this Act shall commence
and take Effect, and be put in Execution, instead of the said recited
Act.

II. And be it further enacted, That upon and from the Commence- Pawnbrokers
ment of this Act, it shall be lawful for all Persons using and exercising allowed to
the Trade or Business of a Pawnbroker, to demand, receive, and take, take certain
                                                                        Rates.
9 O   of

Limits were fixed on charges and other criteria were as follows;

Annual Pawnbrokers license fee	£15
£2 or less (£2000 today)	20pc over 12 months
Over £2 to £10	15pc over 12 months
Flat rate ticket charge up to 4d on loans over half a pound (£1.50 today)	
Unredeemed pledges of less than 10 shillings would be forfeited to the pawnbroker. Unreemed items over 10 shilllings would be sold at auction with any surplus being returned to the pledger.	
Illegal to serve a drunk person (pawnbrokers were often next to pubs and gin palaces- it is alleged that women would often pawn clothing to walk next door for a glass of gin)	

So if you took out a loan of £4 (£4000 today) and redeemed after 6 months you would pay back in today's money a loan charge of £201.50. This of course took pricing competition out of the market to the customer's detriment but stopping the outliers charging extortionate rates was considered to be the greater good.

Another important factor was the introduction of the requirement that for any pawn over 10s (£500 in today's money) any surplus on sale of an unredeemed item must be returned to the original owner. This was rarely publicised and the popular belief amongst the public was that if you don't redeem in time you always lost the item and received no surplus. In practice few people had pawns over the threshold value. This was the topic of vexed argument between John Hollingshead and pawnbroker George Attenborough. Hollingshead argued that pawnbrokers would collude with auctioneers such that bidding would be low and the item returned to the pawnbroker at a knocked down reserve price thereby swindling the customer. Attenborough won the day with the argument that it would not be in the auctioneers best interest as they gained commission on the sale and would earn less if the item didn't sell for the true market price. It was also noted that the average pawn redemption in 1844 was 95%.

Alfred Keeson[17] was another prominent member of the pawnbroking trade in the first half of the 19th century and was highly respected by parliament. His arguments were generally sensible except for one provision. He had argued strongly that clothing should be subject to 6 month pawns and everything else should be 12 months, but it was not clear why he pushed for this. He must have known that in industrial towns a typical pawn of best clothing went in on Monday and out on Saturday, so that best cloths were available for Sunday church, and hence the rhyme;

---

[17] Mont de Piete and Pawnbroking   Alfred Keeson 1854

Half a pound of t'penny rice,
Half a pound of treacle.
That's the way the money goes.
Pop goes the weasel

The above meaning food is what you needed the money for and to get it you would pop (pawn) the weasel (cockney rhyming slang- 'weasel and flute' = suit)

Another interesting phrase developed during the period was 'up the spout'. This referred to the dumb waiter a form of chimney between the ground floor shop and the upstairs warehouse where pawns were stored. If you goods go up this spout and you fail to redeem you may never see them again.

Interestingly, British pawnbrokers were unusual in that they actively lobbied parliamentarians and wanted to be regulated. Pawnbrokers were possibly the first lobbying group in Britain. This was because they saw that having a legal structure set them apart as professionals and that it was a good way of preventing new entrants and charlatans entering the trade and ripping customers off. Their drive of course was that pawnbroking was extremely profitable and they wanted to keep on the right side of Government. One of the key factors was that in reality people only took pawns for a week or two but would have to pay the full months loan charge. People who redeemed after just a few days were paying around 650pc APR for the privilege.

It is probably the introduction of such laws that stopped the development of Charity shop loans (the Monts de Piete which had sprung up elsewhere in Europe) ever establishing a foothold in England. Ireland , however, was a different matter, a series of bodged laws had a serious impact on the relationship between the pawnbroker and his customers and actively encouraged corruption. The Salvation Army proposed a Monts de Piete scheme but nothing ever came of it.

A Case Study in How Not to Legislate?- Ireland

1780 Act Of Usury- Maximum charge for a loan for any period set at 6%

1786 Amendment to Act- No pawn could be for more than £10, tapered interest up to 6%, with the pawnbroker fined for any damage to goods. £300 security was required to trade at all. A monthly return and fees were required and these were paid to the Marshal of Dublin. All un-redemptions must be auctioned by Dublin Auction House (which was 'coincidently' owned by the Marshal).

1788 Amendment to Act- Police were to be responsible for auctions. This led to widespread corruption between pawnbrokers and the police to the detriment of customers. Security to trade increase to £1,800.

Corruption continued into the 19th century. By the 1820's pawnbrokers books were not inspected by the Marshalry so long as £5 was paid in advance annually, Auction sales were conducted in the countryside in the middle of the night and no catalogues were kept.

Meanwhile in England the 1800 Act and its minor amendments worked fairly well , on the whole, for the best part of 75 years, but it was amended during this period on three occasions:-

- 1815: License duties were raised to £15 for London and £7.50 for the country.
- 1840: The reward to the common informer for reporting illegal rates of interest was abolished.
- 1860: The Half Penny Act- The pawnbroker was empowered to charge a halfpenny (15p in today's money) for the pawn-ticket when the loan was under five shillings (£20 in today's money). This was an important victory for pawnbrokers.

The driver for the authorities was that they much preferred customers to use registered professional pawnbrokers than back street , so called, 'dolly shops' or what we would call today illegal loan sharks. If there was not at least some profit in small pawns through a reasonable pawn ticket charge, the pawnbroker would refuse the custom forcing the pawnee to go round the corner to nearby dolly shops where they would certainly be ripped off.

Interestingly, the former adversary of pawnbrokers Mr Charles Dickens, in later life now came down firmly on the side of the pawnbroker;

'It used to be supposed that my Uncle (the pawnbroker) lent to little on the pledges he received; but he can have no motive for so doing, as he speculates on the receipt of interest and the more principal he can safely lend, the more interest he hopes to gain. Moreover there is individual competition in his business, as in all other businesses'[18]

The Act was not however, universally popular. The Pawnbrokers' National Association and the Pawnbrokers Defense Association which together are the forerunners of the modern NPA (National Pawnbrokers Association) worked hard to obtain a revision of the Act. Those presenting to the select committee included Mr John Dicker and Mr Richard Attenborough both longstanding and respected pawnbrokers . It was argued that the usury laws had been abolished for the whole of the community except the pawnbroker. There were no interest restrictions for banks for example. In fact the restrictions on profit were so great that they argued it was not worth lending money on bulky articles requiring storage.

In 1870 the House of Commons held a Select Committee hearing on Pawnbroking. It was stated in evidence that in the previous year nearly 208 million pledges were lodged, of which up to 20% was London based. The average value of pledges appeared to be about 4s. (£16 today), and it was claimed that the proportion of articles pawned dishonestly was found to be only 1 in 14,000. Later official statistics show that of the forfeited pledges sold in London less than 20 per million were claimed by the police.

---

[18] My Uncle Household Words Charles Dickens 1852

1872 Pawnbrokers Act

Select Committee hearings led to the Pawnbrokers Act 1872, which repealed, altered and consolidated all previous legislation on the subject, and is still the basis of more recent legislation which regulates the relations between the public and pawnbrokers. It put an end to the old irritating restrictions, and reduced the annual tax in London from £15 to the £7.50 paid in the provinces. By the provisions of the Act (which does not affect loans above £10):-

- A pledge is redeemable within one year, and seven days of grace added to the year for people to redeem slightly late.

- Pledges pawned for half of one pound or less and not redeemed in time become the property of the pawnbroker. No notice of sale is required. Pawns were generally sold by the pawnbroker in his window.

- Pledges above half of one pound are redeemable until sale, which must be by public auction. Any surplus after loan interest and costs must be returned to the pawnor.

- In addition to one halfpenny (16p today) for the pawn-ticket (sometimes not charged for very small pawns) the pawnbroker is entitled to charge as interest one halfpenny per month on every 2s. or part of 2s. lent (2% per month) where the loan is under £2, and on every 2s. 6d. (1.66% per month) where the loan is above £2 (£150 today).

- Special contracts may be made where the loan is above £2, at a rate of interest agreed on between lender and borrower.

- These made offences punishable by summary conviction:-
  - Unlawful pawning of goods not the property of the pawner.
  - Taking in pawn any article from a person under the age of <u>twelve</u>, or intoxicated.
  - Taking in pawn any linen or apparel or unfinished goods or materials entrusted to wash or repair (this relates to seemstresses and so on, pawning goods they don't own.)
- A new pawnbroker must produce a <u>magistrate</u>'s certificate before he can receive a license.
- The permit cannot be refused if the applicant gives sufficient evidence that he is a person of good character. So long as the person is not a) intoxicated or b) under the age of 12.
- The word "pawnbroker" must always be inscribed in large letters over the door of the shop.
- If an item is thought to be stolen and seized by a constable, the judge can decide to award the pawnbroker compensation.

Following the Irish experience of dodgy auctions in the middle of the night and in the middle of nowhere, elaborate provisions were made to safeguard the interests of borrowers whose unredeemed pledges would be sold under the act. Specifically auctions could only take place only on the first Monday of January, April, July and October.

The maximum allowable loan on a pawn ticket was £10 and the term of the contract was 12 months. The annual interest on loans of 2s. had been increased by successive acts of parliament as follows;

Annual Interest on a 2s loan by Act of Parliament	
1784	6%
1800	20%
1872	25%

In Scotland, the Law regarding pawnbroking echoed English Law. By the mid 1800s there were around 300 pawnbrokers in Edinburg and Glasgow alone. For some inexplicable reason a pawn ticket cost a penny in Scotland rather than a halfpenny in English law. Interestingly the standard term for a pawn was set at 6 months which was later copied by English Law.

A good analysis of Pawnbroking Law was published by pawnbroker Charles Attenborough with input from John Attenborough- solicitor in 1987[19]

A good deal of the principals of the 1872 Act remain in place today, despite minor updates in 1922, (which allowed a document fee of a halfpence per multiple of 5 shillings loan) and further Acts in 1960, the 1974 Consumer Credit Act and the 2010 Consumer Credit Directive from the European Parliament.

---

[19] The Law of Pawnbroking, Charles L Attenborough 1897

BOURNEMOUTH COUNTY BOROUGH COUNCIL

P.L.

£7   10s.   Od.

No. 36

PAWNBROKER'S LICENCE

Messrs George D. Barns + Son Ltd,
742, Christchurch Road,
Boscombe,
Bournemouth.

Granted at the Office of the Controller of Licences at
†The Town Hall, Bournemouth, on the 24th July, 1957

I, the undersigned, duly authorised by the Bournemouth
County Borough Council, hereby grant Licence to the above-
named (‡) to exercise and carry on the Business of a
PAWNBROKER in a shop specified above (*) from the
date hereof until and including the 21st July 1958.

_____, the sum of SEVEN POUNDS TEN
SHILLINGS having been paid for this Licence.

pp Douglas Taylor.

COUNTY BOROUGH OF BOURNEMOUTH

THE PAWNBROKERS ACT, 1872.

WE, THE MAYOR ALDERMEN AND BURGESSES OF THE BOROUGH OF BOURNEMOUTH do hereby certify that we do authorise the grant to GEO. A. PAYNE AND SON LIMITED whose registered office is situate at 742 Christchurch Road Boscombe in the County Borough of Bournemouth of a licence to carry on the business of Pawnbrokers at 742 Christchurch Road within the said Borough

WITNESS THE COMMON SEAL of THE MAYOR ALDERMEN AND BURGESSES OF THE BOROUGH OF BOURNEMOUTH this Second day of July One thousand nine hundred and fifty-seven:-

W. P. M. Lewis

Town Clerk

1960 Act

Although the laws were well received, the key problem with the 1872 Act was its inflexibility. Enshrining the interest rate in law assumes everything stays the same (what economists would call 'ceteris parabis'). However, as explored in subsequent chapters, profits were falling after the Great War as costs rose. A hundred pawnbrokers a year went out of business in the 1940s alone. According to Customs and Excise (the forerunner of HMRC) there were 3384 pawnbrokers in the UK in 1931 and only 1726 pawnbrokers by 1949

By the late 1950's with the introduction of the welfare state the number and also value of pawns had fallen such that the average net profit was around 3%[20] . No pawnbroker was making much money. In many case clerical costs of servicing pawns outweighed the interest value of them. Something had to be done.

The 1960 Act resulted from the very hard work of the National Pawnbrokers Association who drafted the Act from 1955 and submitted it to the Select Committee to review. When presented as a bill to parliament it passed through parliament and became in Act in 13 weeks flat.

The NPA found it had some very influential friends in the House of Lords –Sir Graham Page and Lord Meston who between them drove the Bill through respective Houses of Parliament.

Meston is quoted in Hansard as saying;

---

[20] The Decline of Pawnbroking A Minkes Feb 1953

"Unless we do something to help dear old Uncle he will rapidly go out of business altogether. How would your lordships like to be remunerated on the same basis you were in 1872?"

He went on to show that with capital of £5,000 and avergae receipts of £1,250 a pawnbroker would have to employ a manager, and 2 assistants plus rent , rates, insurance and utilities. He speculated that there was very little profit left for the average pawnbroker.

The 1960 Act updated previous Acts and achieved the following;

-Increased the limit of any one pledge from £10 to £50.

-Another aspect of the act was to reduce the contract term from 12 months to 6 months

-Allowed that pawns for loans under £2 were automatically forfeited to the pawnbroker if not redeemed. Unredeemed pawns on loans up to £5 were required to be auctioned and above this level the pawnbroker could make a special agreement to sell in their shop window instead (to be known as a private treaty).

The effect was immediate and probably saved the profession; pawnbrokers immediately received new clientele from the more affluent middle classes. They had previously borrowed on unsecured loans at 48% and were only too keen to switch to pawnbroking at 25%.

1974 Consumer Credit Act

The 1960 Act kept the industry alive but in intensive care. The problem now switched to the artificial limit of 25% per annum interest which had been set using 1872 economics as a yardstick and never updated. The National Pawnbrokers Association lobbied and produced a draft Bill to increase this rate. The Government were interested in this but had a bigger goal to overhaul the law affecting the whole of the Consumer Credit Industry. This was a significant shift, never again would laws be made just for Pawnbrokers but the industry was now considered a subset of the shole consumer credit market. The Government carried out its own research of 20% of the pawnbroking market using NOP Market Research Ltd.[21] Key findings were as follows;

1	Most pawnbrokers had been in business for more than 20 years and very few new entrants
2	60% are Limited Companies 40% Sole Traders
3	20% lent unsecured loans
4	90% did something else such as jewellery sales, general retailing (cameras)
5	Average low pledge 22s 6d, Average Mid pledge £3 10s , Average Special Contract £12 10s
6	10% of pledges were immediately renewed
7	50% pawned to pay immediate bills , the rest were for holidays, weddings or to buy goods

[21] Consumer Credit: Money Lenders and Pawnbrokers- Report of the Crowther Committee Vol 1, July 1970

The Consumer Credit Act 1974, introduced by Geoffrey Howe, was finally approved by Parliament at the end of July, following input from the Crowther Commission. It covered a wide range of credit activities and repealed the Pawnbroking Acts of 1872 and 1960 as well as previous Moneylenders' Acts in UK and Ireland.

Interestingly the Act became law immediately but certain sections including pawnbroking, or pledging, would only come into force at a future date- anticipated to be in 1983 because practical details, including the wording of contracts need to be agreed between the NPA and OFT (Office of Fair Trading).

In general terms the Act laid down for all credit;

-The need to show the true cost to the customer of the credit provided

-What items are involved

-The method of calculating the rate of charge

The key provisions of the Act included;

License from OFT	The Pawnbroker, as with other credit providers would need to have a license from the Office of Fair Trading (OFT) and to demonstrate they are fit and proper businesses.
Advertisements	All Financial Promotions must conform to subsequent

	Regulations. The customer must not be misled.
Canvassing	The Pawnbroker can only trade from their premises and not, for example, door to door.
Pre Contract information and withdrawal	The contract must be described to the customer before the Contract is presented to them to sign. The customer must be advised they have 14 days to change their mind and withdraw from the contract (S66A) and that there are consequences of failure to redeem.
Creditworthiness assessment	Crucially the act states in section 55B (4b) that pawns are to be excluded from any such assessment requirement. Customers could be chased for debt beyond the sale value of the item.
Contracts (Pawnbroking is a fixed sum credit agreement)	The customer must be given a copy of the contract. Contracts must state- The amount of credit, the duration of contract, and interest payable. The term was to be at least 6

	months or longer and the customer could redeem any day within this period, or beyond it if the goods had not been sold by the Pawnbroker. The redemption interest rate post contract was to be no greater than the rate during the contract.
	If you lost your pawn contract you could still redeem but would need a statutory declaration from a lawyer. (This repealed the probvision in the 1873 Act that stated that anyone with the pawn ticket could redeem the goods)
Non redemption	If you failed to redeem and the loan was for £15 (now £75) or less the item will be forfeited, however if for £15(now £75) or more then the customer retains title and any surplus after capital, interest, and reasonable costs would be returned to the customer.
Maximum Pawn	The maximum pawn on one ticket rose to pledges of £5,000

This was helpful in enshrining in law the best practice relating to contracts and customer care.

2010 Consumer Credit Directive EU

The 1974 Act was the best piece of legislation to date and was responsible for reducing bad practice. It also encouraged growth in NPA membership as a result. Joining the common market (EU) had little impact at this time and relations between the trade and the OFT were broadly cordial with both parties keen to stamp out bad practice and 'loan sharks'.

During this period customers felt they knew where they stood. Interest rates were expressed as a percentage per month, typically between 5% and 10% even when inflation was at 16% in the 1980's. Roughly 3% of the public used pawnbrokers and they understood that the rate for the month was fixed, so whether you redeemed on say 4th of the month or 27th of the month the rate was fixed.

The European parliament decided that they needed to create a level playing field so that the customer could survey borrowing options and determine the best product for them, and further that the interest rate had to be expressed in the same way regardless of the type of loan. They therefore commissioned mathematicians to create a standard calculation called the APR (annual percentage rate) based on the theoretical period of one year.

This sounds sensible at a basic level until one tries to implement such a calculation (see chapter 2). Firstly a pawnbroking loan is for 6 or 7 months only, so in factoring this up to a full year you are portraying a level of interest that would never ever be charged. Similarly the rate of a mortgage is based on say 25 years, so to reduce this to a nominal one is a work of fiction because if it were a one year loan the bank would charge a considerably higher rate. Another factor is that pawnbrokers have to build all other costs charged into the APR calculation whereas banks do not have to.

It is incomprehensible to compare the rate of interest of a 25 year mortgage loan of say £200,000 with a 6 month loan of £50. When you factor down the compound interest of a 25 year loan to one year it will look exceedingly small whereas the grossed up short term loan will look massive. As discussed previously it is like comparing the cost of a one mile taxi drive with the cost of a flight to New York. Obviously per mile the taxi will be more, but you can't get a plane to take you one mile.

The result of all this is that what used to be a very simple and understandable calculation for customers has become implausibly complex. For example previously let's assume a customer had borrow £100 for 6 months at a rate of 6% per month, if they redeemed anytime in the first month they would pay back £106, anytime in the second month they would pay £112 and so on.

The 2010 directive states that the customer must be advised the APR. The APR of 6% a month would be 85.0% APR. Not surprisingly when a customer is faced with this incomprehensible figure they will typically just say – how much is that a month? Answer- £6. The customer would typically respond 'well why didn't you just say that in the first place, that's fine.'

The second important aspect of the Directive was that if someone wished to redeem then they would be charged daily compounded interest. Consequently the cost at redemption changes daily not monthly. However since the contract has technically been broken by the act of redeeming the Directive states that compensation is due to the pawnbroker. That is to say that the customer should really give 28 days' notice of intention to redeem. Almost no customers do this, they generally want their pawn back immediately and are therefore prepared to pay a penalty of up to 28 days. Consequently, in our example, someone redeeming on the 29th day of the second month one would previously have paid £12. After this Directive they would pay anything between £110.55 and £115.84 depending on the benevolence of the pawnbroker.

The problem with the complexity of the calculation of APRs and the daily interest calculations immediately led to two outcomes;

a)   It was impossible to be a pawnbroker any more without sophisticated software and many businesses were sold when their owners retired.

b)   Very few people understood the calculations and what an APR really meant.

With regards to the latter point, this had a major impact on unsecured loans. In the case of such loans money lenders would be taking significantly more risk than pawnbroking because the loan had no security to back it. In finance, risk equals cost, so not surprisingly in taking the chance that you lend the money and the person disappears, the lender is going to want a much higher rate of interest. So a loan designed for 2 weeks when factored up for an imaginary year would show an APR of 1000's of percent. Neither the media nor most politicians understood this calculation and consequently quoted high APRs as being outrageous. They were of course quoting annualised compound rates and not the true interest rate. To use an extreme example, if I borrowed 5 pounds from you and paid it back the next day and bought you a drink as a thank you, we would both think that was reasonable. The monetary equivalent of this would represent an APR of close to infinity.

The problem was further compounded by the requirement to give new customers a SECCI (Standard European Consumer Credit Information). Again this was a one size fits all document with very very small print that had all the details regarding the contract you were shortly to be shown. This document, designed for mortgages, had to be shown to all new customers or those who hadn't been in the store for 3 years or more. NPA Research has shown that very few customers are interested in the document, and cannot understand why they are being presented with this small print prior to receiving the contract to look at which bears exactly the same information.

The EU legislators assumption is that all this information helps the customer make an informed decision. Well no-one is making a decision based on a choice between £100 from a pawnbroker or a 25 year mortgage of £100. And in terms of comparing one pawnbroker to another, the EU assumption ignores all the other factors. Top of the list is trust. If I am intrusting a family heirloom to the safe of a pawnbroker I am going to want to know I can trust them not to lose it and that their security is robust. I am therefore likely to use the pawnbroker I trust again and again. I am unlikely to go down the road to an untried and untested pawnbroker to save half a per cent of interest.

Finally, adverts and financial promotions needed to quote APRs, and if trigger words like 'best rates' were used this would trigger the need to show an example.

Perhaps the greatest irony of all was that the EU legislators, the Office of Fair Trading, and the NPA all thought that when the law was implemented by each market, that the UK, like all the others, would exempt pawnbroking on the basis that as a secured loan it is not comparable to all other forms of lending. Unfortunately the newly elected Conservative Liberal Democrat alliance, stated that there would be no exemptions whatsoever for those involved in Consumer Credit. This ill thought through judgement has had significant implications on the UK pawnbroker.

2014 Financial Conduct Authority Regime

Following political pressure to deal with the issue of what the media saw as outrageous interest rates of unsecured loans (by misunderstanding APR calculations), called in common parlance 'Pay

Day Loans', and a common feeling that the OFT did not have enough teeth to pursue rogue traders and loan sharks, the Government combined the Consumer Credit activities of the OFT with the Financial Services Authority to create a new Financial Conduct Authority. This had the impact of most of the OFT staff transferring to FCA offices in Canary Wharf, London. Consequently an organisation created to deal with banks and very large financial firms, suddenly had to deal with 60,000 very small firms, mostly akin to family corner shops.

The regime was tasked with taking the 1974 Consumer Credit Act and it's subsequent amendments, and the Consumer Credit Directive 2010, and turn these into a rule book called CONC (The Consumer Credit Sourcebook).

Chapter 5- Pre-Industrial Revolution and The Victorian Era

The first references to a pawnbrokers shop are in Berwick in 1598 and Stony Stratford in 1624. The trade was regulated locally at this time. Local towns banned pawnbroking without a license as an official broker. The rules were, you must be of good standing and keep records of all transactions. Pawn as a term goes back to 1496 according to the Oxford English Dictionary. It isn't known how the lower classes would have talked about the process but we do know what the upper classes would have said. The poplar parlance was – 'I'm going to lay my xxxx in lavender'. Popular items were plates and jewellery being valuable items of the day.

Pawnbroking tended to be an urban phenomenon because in towns there was a ready market to dispose of unredeemed pawns and a flow of customers to make the enterprise worthwhile. London in the seventeenth century had a population of some 200,000, a town like Nottingham had less than 10,000 inhabitants.

Pawnbroking grew as the towns grew by providing liquidity to land owners and to some extent enterprise in the shape of businesses like cloth making, farming and building. By the 18th century, perhaps like the modern example of Pay Day loans, the pawnbrokers and goldsmiths were beginning to price themselves out of the markets. As a reaction against the greed of around 80% APR in a market with minimal inflation, James II set up a charity with the snappy title "The Charitable Corporation for Lending Money to the Industrious but Necessitous Poor" which was basically a version of the Italian *montes pietas* and was publically funded. Pawnbrokers rapidly declined for the next 24 years until the charity went spectacularly out of bust as we mentioned in the previous chapter.

This brought a change in fortune for Pawnbrokers as the public reached the conclusion you can't trust a charity in the way you can trust an honest businessman who trades on his reputation. By 1750 in London alone there were 250 large shops and over 300 smaller ones.

Perhaps with the thought of the corrupt charity in mind the larger pawnbrokers decided to pull together and use their new influence in society to lobby for a law that would outlaw the outliers- those smaller businesses that were not observing good practice. To be fair there may have been an element of protectionism given the rate at which the market was growing and with few barriers to entry. The availability of free cash being the primary one.

This activity culminated in the introduction of a bill to Parliament for the larger pawnbrokers to protect themselves against the equally snappily named;

Introduction of the Three Balls Symbol

It was at this point that the three balls became used as a sign of compliance with the Act. It is certainly true that the three balls came from the bottom half of the Medici bankers logo, and were originally the blue colour of that logo. In all probability the balls became gold because gold was seen as more prestigious by the goldsmiths who engaged in pawnbroking. One myth that is incorrect is the idea that the two level balls indicated that there is a 2 to 1 chance you wont get your items back is not correct. Redemptions are typically much higher and in modern times are in excess of 85%.

The Poor

Compassion for the poor was however somewhat limited. In 1796 Patrick Colquhoun[22] wrote that the habit of pawnbroking was exceedingly widespread with more than 240 pawnbrokers in London and castigated London's poor for improvidence. When they weren't working they were drinking and chattering in public houses, if they ran out of money they pawned coal at night and redeemed the coal in the morning in exchange for the blankets they slept in. Indeed most of the customers were poor as Colquhoun observed, pawnbroking was the 'habit' of London's poor and 'if these modes of raising money were not accessible.....thousands would unavoidably perish in the streets' .

Dickens maintained that pawnbrokers were the bankers for the poor. A journalist in the 1860's refers to the people falling down the platforms to the bottom of the social system, and hence the phrase 'spiralling debt'

---

[22] A Treatise on Indulgence Patrick Colquhoun 1796

Statistics	1830	1851	1870
Number of Pawnbrokers	London 380 Rest of England +Wales 1096 Scotland <u>61</u> Total 1537	London 366 Rest of England and Wales 4,367	London 580
Number of Pledges	6 million		208 million
Average loan	5d (£15 today)		4s (£16 today)
Employed in Pawnbroking	>5000		
Average redemptions	95%		
Stolen Items pawned			Negligible (20 per million)

Whereas pawnbroking began as a tool for the rich and kings to raise money, by the nineteenth century the focus had most definitely moved to the poor who pawned out of necessity. This was exacerbated by the migration into the great towns and cities of the industrial revolution. The Victorian reaction from the establishment was typically unforgiving. The poor should be castigated for their thoughtlessness and lack of frugality in racking up debt. Indeed no end of moralists lined up to tell them to sort themselves out. A person who borrowed 3d (£1) a week would be paying 850% interest in a year. It was felt that ruin and desolation would follow, however, there was little evidence of the writing classes providing any helpful ideas as to how such a poor family could get themselves out of their debt spiral. But what were they pawning? An analysis of most pawned items by the British Association for the Advancement of Science[23] who studied a Glasgow pawnbrokers came up with the following list in 1836;

1836 Most Pawned Items	
Womens gowns	32%
Petticoats	9%
Mens Coats	9%
Vests	6%
Sheets	5%
Shirts	5%
Trousers	5%
Bedcovers	4%
Silk hankies	4%
Watches	3%
Rings	3%
Blankets	3%

[23] Pawnbroking Establishments in England and the Continent Knights Penny Magazine Vol 5 1836

Interestingly 48 Waterloo Medals were amongst the stock.

Rings and watches are surprisingly low on the list suggesting that the average pawn was of low value. The estimated average pawn value in England and France in 1833 was 15d (£5 in today's money), and 78% were redeemed, a further 17% were renewed and only 5% were sold.2 million pledges were made per year in London alone. There were 1,537 registered and licensed pawnbrokers in Britain of which 380 were in London.

Advice for and castigation of the poor continued unabated for most of the century, and yet most advise was given not directly to the poor but shared in the media such as the Times and Penny magazine. It is certain that the majority of the audience they were offering 'advice' to would not have seen it, since most would not have been able to read or right let alone waste precious resources on buying a newspaper. The Penny Magazine stated that the poor wasted money on 'momentary and unprofitable gratification'. For the middle classes to hire workers for a pittance and then lambast them for not being able to make ends meet was Victorian hypocrisy at its worst.

Pawnbrokers were time and again pointed out in the media and by some authorities as fences for stolen goods, however, it was considered opinion that experienced criminals would not use pawnbrokers but to 'professional fences' . Gatrell and Hadden[24] carried out a study of criminal statistics and stated that the most likely thieves who used pawnbrokers were;

[24] Criminal Statistics and Their Interpretation Gatrell and Hadden 1972

Mechanics and labourers	Stolen flat irons and tools
Middle aged women	Stolen sheets and clothing from washing lines
Butlers	Silver plate to provide funds for betting on horses
Out of work builders, plumbers, carpenters	Stealing tools of the trade
Lodgers	Stealing from the landlord

There were also various tricks at play to fool the pawnbroker. The most popular cons were developed by Duffers. Duffers, who were nearly always women, would sweet talk the pawnbroker, take out a pawn with a genuine article, redeem it and then having gained his trust, would substitute the item for a similar looking low quality item and pawn it. This time the pawnbroker wouldn't examine the coat as he believed it to be the original coat. The Duffer would take the money and disappear leaving the pawnbroker out of pocket.

There is no doubt that typical customers were working class but many were also traders and small businessmen who all had lack of access to banks as a common factor.

By the end of the Victorian era, the image of the pawnbroker had changed. The profession was becoming much better accepted and the 'Dolly Shop' or illegal back street traders had largely been wiped out.

The work of the Pawnbrokers Association which became the National Pawnbrokers Association in 1892 had been to establish the industry as a provider of good service and subject to proper rule of law and regulation. We shall return to the NPA in later chapters.

Chapter 6   The National Pawnbrokers Association

The NPA was founded in 1892 and incorporated in 1931 as a company limited by guarantee. In June 1989, with the benefit of almost a century of experience, it reviewed and re-wrote its original constitution. The review had several purposes, but was undertaken in particular:

- to take account of the expansion of the pawnbroking industry
- to ensure that its affairs and those of its members were more efficiently regulated
- to protect the public interest

The NPAs values are fairness and transparency, professionalism and excellence, and expertise. All members are bound by rules and by a customer code of conduct which they sign up to annually. Nearly all pawnbrokers are members of the NPA. The logo is proudly displayed in stores and on websites and contracts. This chapter shows how the Association came about.

Throughout the 1800's pawnbrokers were somewhat punch drunk with continued efforts to undermine them, either by parliamentarians trying to pass draconian laws or short lived competition from well-meaning charities which consistently failed but provided short term competition for the pawnbroker. If you over lend at low interest for charitable reasons it no surprise, human nature being what it is, that you are unlikely to see the customer or the money again and people who like to do good do not see themselves as debt collectors when things go wrong.

As early as the 1700's there had been collectives, and loose societies based on common need and perspective amongst the pawnbrokers. These communities started to crystalize with the drive towards the 1800 Act. By 1821 London Pawnbrokers had successfully organised themselves into a protectionist union called the Pawnbrokers' Institution which was part of the Pawnbrokers Society. The National Pawnbrokers Association have the original signed copy of the 1821 Society rulebook which was their foundation document (below).

Below are the first ever minutes of the 1821 Society with Mr J C
Harrison in the chair and 46 members in attendance.

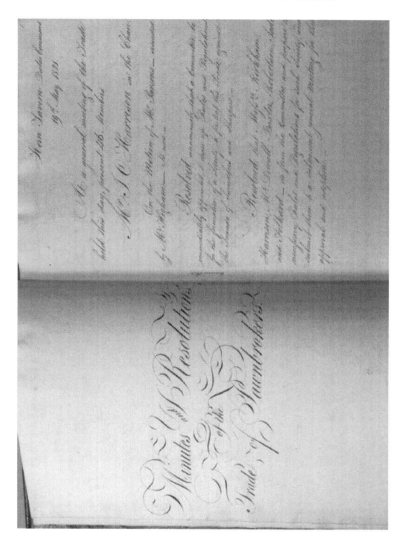

The rules were clearly focused on differentiating Pawnbrokers in the
Society from those who were not, and specifically those in the trade

who were basically crooks engaging in sharp practice, and those customers who were engaging in fraud or deceptions of "Swindlers and Sharpers"

The Society of Pawnbrokers
Established
For protecting themselves against the Frauds
of
Swindlers and Sharpers

Rules and Regulations

1st. That a Society, consisting of Pawnbrokers only (and such Gentleman as have retired from the Business) be formed, for detecting and prosecuting any person or persons who shall practice any imposition on the Trade; and preventing as much as possible the daily frauds taking place with a continuation of success by giving such public as the nature of the case may require.

2nd. That the Society will in no case allow any part of its Fund to be applied for the purpose of defending and protecting any of its Members in taking illegal interest, or who in any other manner shall offer against

The Pawnbrokers' Association was formed in 1836, and these two bodies (the Society and the Association) decided to combine in 1847 and called themselves the snappily named- Metropolitan United Pawnbrokers' Protection Society (MUPPS).

One of the key reasons to combine resources was to fight an invasive private members bill. Basically any parliamentarian can propose a bill and if it gets enough traction can be taken on board and occasionally a bill will reach the statute book. In 1844 an MP called W F Cowper tried to pass a private members bill – the Charitable Pawn Societies Bill[25] which would have made pawnbroking illegal. Fortunately this impractical suggestion came to nought thanks to the lobbying of the two bodies.

By the 1860s things had considerably picked up and the Association was gathering steam in respect of most pawnbrokers, especially in London, happy to join and the Association proved it was happy to face challenges from government and legislators head on. However other local Associations continued alone. One of the biggest gripes was pawnbrokers being lumped in with Marine Stores, Wardrobe Dealers and other back street second hand stores, as being 'fences' and generally characters of ill repute. This is despite statistics which were available to the House of Commons Select Committee from 1970 which showed only one in every 14,000 pledges could be proven to be stolen. Indeed in 1882 F.Mabel Robinson[26] revealed

25 Law of Pawnbroking Levine

that out of 6 million forfeited pledges sold in London in that year only 96 items were sought by the police.

The pawnbrokers were keen to lobby parliament to have a Pawnbrokers Act that would differentiate the legal law abiding pawnbroker from illegal traders. As we have seen in previous chapters , this concluded in the 1872 Pawnbrokers Act. Pawnbrokers were possibly the first lobbying group in Britain. This was because they saw that having a legal structure set them apart as professionals and that it was a good way of preventing new entrants and charlatans entering the trade and ripping customers off. Their drive of course was that pawnbroking was extremely profitable and they wanted to keep on the right side of Government. One of the key factors was that in reality people only took pawns for a week or two but would have to pay the full month's loan charge. People who redeemed after just a few days were paying around 650pc APR for the privilege.

By 1872 the Pawnbrokers Association working with other Associations, came together to form a committee of pawnbrokers to shape the 1872 Pawnbrokers Bill and they handed their documentation to the parliamentary select committee. After the implementation of the Act the various societies worked slightly more closely together through the Pawnbrokers Gazette which had started life in 1838. Here through anecdotal tales of the life of pawnbrokers and customers up and down the country, there were common interests, complaints and focus expressed. Even the adverts have historical interest.

[26] Pawnbroking in England and Abroad Robinson 1882

Formation of the NPA in Derby in 1892

But what was required was an umbrella body to head a federation of societies and focus specific action principally with the government, in the interests of protecting all pawnbrokers. The leading crusader to keep a permanent national association was a Liverpool man , Alfred Hardaker, who campaigned for 20 years to create a National Pawnbrokers Association. In 1892 he succeeded. With support from the appropriately named John Goolden they first persuaded the Newcastle & Gateshead Pawnbrokers Association they together lobbied Associations up and down the country.

The inaugural meeting was hosted by the Mechanics Institute in Derby on 8th June 1892[27]. It was decided they would meet as a national committee every 3 years and retain their interests in their local societies, but that all local Associations would merge and co-ordinate activities under the federal banner of the NPA. Hardaker acted as the very first secretary to the NPA and held the post for 3 years, but retired due to ill health in favour of James Sprunt. A set of rules were drawn up but these proved short lived and inadequate. An argument over fees ensued and the Metropolitan Pawnbrokers Protection Society refused to join and pay the 2s 6d member fee. (they finally joined 3 years later). The fee had been designed to give the Association an annual income of £120 and £50 for reserves.

---

[27] Souvenir of the 14th Triennial Meeting, NPA, Edinburgh, May 26th 1937

The NPA was formed as a federal body controlling no less than 16 Pawnbrokers Protection Societies covering England, Scotland, and Northern Ireland. The largest was London Metropolitan and the smallest Bristol and Portsmouth societies.

Their triennial meetings were events in themselves as the programme from 1937 attests;

Tuesday May 25, 1937   Day- Meeting at Station Hotel , Edinburgh

                    Evening- Civic Reception by Lord Provost

Wednesday May 26   Day- Meeting

                    Evening- Banquet, ladies welcome in evening dress

Thursday May 27   Members will 'entrain' at 9am for journey to Gourock where they will board the steamer 'Duchess of Hamilton' and cruise around the Lochs and Isle of Bute. Lunch and tea served on the steamer

By the end of it's first year the NPA boasted 19 affiliated Societies and 663 members. It took until 1894 to thrash out the rules and agree that Honorary Officers should come from London to avoid the problems of communication by post. By 1898 after the death of Mr Hardaker, the Council met at the Holborn Restaurant and reported 1,721 members and 36 Societies. The total worth was £362. The Council was increased from 5 to 7 members- 1 of which had to be from Scotland and 1 from Ireland.

One of the first tangible benefits was to construct a deal for pawnbrokers to insure their premises and stock with The Goldsmiths and General Burglary Insurance Association. The second was to try to improve the image of the pawnbroker. In the 1890's the Gazette published case studies of leading pawnbrokers showing them to be good citizens from highly professional backgrounds and boasting mayors, alderman, high ranking ex army, and men with good social conscience. The NPA became more aggressive challenging journalists and anyone writing about the profession in a negative way based on prejudice, ignorance, assumptions and lack of evidence or research.

The subsequent years were good for pawnbrokers. The gold price was rising, pawn trade was increasing and there developed a get rich quick feel to the market. By the turn of the century there was a scenario of 'get rich quick' about the market, and many newcomers and existing pawnbrokers did. This surge would not be repeated for 100 years.

1899 Stolen Goods Bill- Success for NPA

The first challenge to the NPA was reduce the impact of what was seen as a draconian bill limiting the activities of pawnbroking. A delegation was sent to Sir Howard Vincent MP and 12 days later the bill was dropped.

1905 The Great Debate

By 1905 the surge was in the post peak period and the NPA petitioned its members to establish if pawnbroking was on the decline. The reaction was mixed. Things were certainly not as good as they had been but demand was still there. One of the factors had been the growth of corporate business who had taken advantage of the new Limited Liability Companies Acts. The largest was Harvey and Thompson Ltd which produced a standard dividend of 10 to 12 per cent every year for decades.

Old Walworth Rd, London

1910 The JP Scandal

Many pawnbrokers were also JPs as they clearly felt it important to be recognised as part of the community and no doubt thought they could add value. In the last quarter of the 19th Century 70 pawnbrokers had been elected to the Bench. In 1908 the Lord Chancellor decreed that no pawnbrokers were to be elected to the Bench any more, which annoyed the NPA tremendously. No justification was ever given. In fact it made no difference because anyone wishing to become a JP simply called themselves a jeweller or general retailer. The prejudice was never policed.

1914- The Great War Years

Times were tough as the war ensued, before the war Monday mornings and Saturday nights were always the busiest times, with women pawning the best suits and clothing on Mondays and redeeming Saturday evening ready for church on Sunday. Meanwhile the man would be busy spending his wages down the pub after a hard weeks work. The liquor Control Board wanted to reduce heavy drinking at the weekend because it interfered with industrial production for the war effort, and so banned alcohol sales from Friday lunchtime to Monday lunchtime. The working class clever way around this was to buy the bottle of spirit Friday morning and pawn it and call in everyday for a slug of alcohol and make a part payment until it had all gone, such that neither the government nor their wives were any the wiser. Not for the first time the NPA sided with the Government and encouraged pawnbrokers to not take alcohol in pawn.

By 1916 the NPA had assets of £13,444 invested, had 2039 members and 1050 individual subscribers.

1922 Act

When members met for the 8th triennial in 1919 after the war, it was agreed that NPA considered the provisions of the 1872 were obsolete and an obstacle to making a just and profitable living. A Committee of 10 were appointed to consider evidence and make an appeal to Parliament for revision of the Act. The Committee was led by Charles Attenborough, since had written a seminal text on the Law of Pawnbroking[28] Unfortunately the report they delivered to members had the unanimous backing of the Committee members but was broadly rejected by the membership. A second Committee was formed and again the membership rejected it. In desperation the NPA left it to the Secretary Sidney Smith to draft the document. He suggested introducing a document fee of one penny per each 5 shillings lent or part thereof (about 2% charge on an average pawn. This was approved almost unanimously (20 members voted against which was 1%).

Parliament accepted the Bill as drafted by NPA but changed the charge to a halfpenny rather than a penny as a sop to the socialist party. This was perhaps Sidney Smith's crowning glory as 2 years later he had to retire due to ill health, although this doesn't seem to have prevented him from becoming President a few years later.

---

[28] The Law of Pawnbroking, Charles L Attenborough 1897

The cost of the Bill drafting was just £300 against a budget of £3,000 and went through all parliamentary stages and in to law in just 58 days. The budget had ben raised by a levy on all members and it was agreed that the balance could be used by NPA as it saw fit.

1925- Lombard Street and Walter Bull

One of the all-time greatest names in pawnbroking is that of Walter Bull. He was President of the Association from 1913 to 1925. He only stopped being President because of ill health and he died aged 87 in 1927. He was responsible for the building of the NPAs offices at Lombard House in Lombard Street, Little Britain, London in 1925 at a cost of £13,494 16s 6d, which came from donations but mostly from Walter Bull himself. This was considered the 3rd most important event for the NPA at the time with first being the 1872 Act and second being the 1922 Act. The crowning moment of his career was opening the board room doors for the first time to much applause on 27th October 1925, and then subsequently passing the building and the Association into the good care of incoming President Sidney Smith.

LOMBARD HOUSE.

How to get to Lombard House

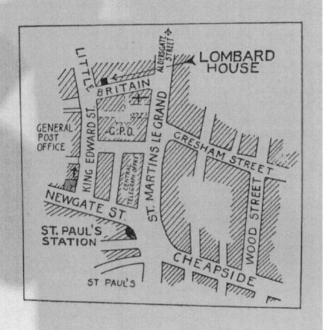

Apart from the building the other legacy of Walter Bull was the Presidents badge which he gave the Association in 1914- massive 18 carat gold trefoil shape. The central figure is St Nicholas the patron saint of pawnbrokers, who holds the gospel in his left hand with the 3 gold balls of pawnbroking. The rose, shamrock and thistle are added to show the coverage of the NPA. Wales was still not covered.

On 12th February 1927 Walter Bull died aged 87 and a bronze plaque was placed opposite his portrait in Lombard House.

This portrait of Walter Bull painted by George Harcourt, was donated by the NPA to the Guildhall Art Gallery in 1973.

Sidney Smith his successor as President (below)had 3 brothers in the clergy and was very religious himself. One of his sons was also a vicar.

Incorporation

The 11ᵗʰ Triennial in 1928 with £19,584 in reserves and 42 affiliated societies, it was agreed that NPA should aim to become incorporated under the forthcoming Companies Act 1929. They had also considered applying for Royal Charter but decided against it. The incorporation was successful and the new Articles of Association came into effect from April 1931. The immediate effect of this was the creation of a new badge, and window stickers with the new logo which could be displayed in stores.

Two other matters of note occurred in the late 1930's, firstly the NPA in 1935 had considered whether they should run an advertising campaign to promote pawnbroking. A ballot of members was not in favour and so the plans were cancelled. Secondly in 1937 the Council agreed that Honorary Officer roles should be eligible to the provinces. Up to this point the Presidency had been controlled by London pawnbrokers.

The Between War Years

The 1920s and 30s saw a slump in business, even despite the great depression of the 30's when traditionally pawnbrokers might have expected to benefit. This was blamed on a number of factors and the Association implored pawnbrokers to find ways of attracting the children of their traditional customers and to seek new customers from the better off in society by advertising, by making their stores more appealing, increasing interest rates and speeding up service. The NPA also claimed with some justification that they were the most controlled of all trades and professions.

The NPA continued to represent nationally on key issues, but it was the strength and comradery of the societies around the country that was the glue that held the body together. The photographs below show examples of the Northern Friendly Society which celebrated their centenary in 1937, ironically with a dinner in Holborn London, close to the home of the NPA.

The other key issue was the continuing problem of fraud, misrepresentation and deception. One notable case featured 3 'actresses who worked in tandem with a crook called Lewis Waller. The women pawned items they didn't own and then Waller appeared to claim them back. Yorkshireman with a business in London Victoria, Mr Thomas Miller Sutton and the Robertson family both traditional pawnbrokers were both defrauded. The court found in their favour shortly before Mr Suttons death in 1934. Many years later the 2 companies were merged into Suttons and Robertsons, which still exist in London today, albeit owned by the Canadian parent company of The Money Shop.

To this day the NPA continues to fight against this scam, with one person pawning the item and an accomplice appearing later to say they own the item. Thankfully this is now covered by 'Fraud by False Representation' under section 1 and 2 of the Fraud Act 2006. Both the pawnor and the accomplice can be charged by police.

But the NPA was not always on the side of the angels. One bizarre passage was the Children's Bill of 1932 which had a clause stating that it would be illegal for children under 16 to make a pledge. The Association fought tooth and nail to stop this but failed.

1940s to 1960s

During this period pawnbroking declined phenomenally and the NPA had its work cut out just keeping afloat. The period is known as the time of the slow death of the pawnbroker. Austerity, changing clientele, growth of the economy in the post war years, the fixed gold price and the welfare state made it very difficult for the pawnbroker to make money, and many small pawnbrokers felt increasingly squeezed out by the larger chains. To illustrate the point according to NPA archives very dramatically, in 1900 there were 1,488 members but by 1980 there were 115 members a 92% decline. Many pawnbrokers simply retired, others focused on jewellery and second hand activity.

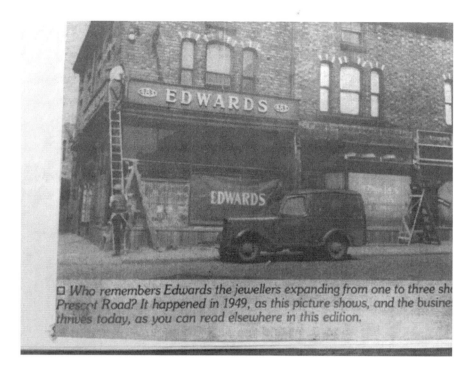

W J Edwards, Old Swan, Liverpool, 1949

In the late fifties the NPA campaign hard for a new Act to raise the pawn limit from £10 to £50. A team of 4 Council members drafted a Bill, engaged government and researched the market as well as encouraging pawnbrokers to lobby their local MPs. The 1960 Pawnbroking Act did make this change and improved business. The contract period was also reduced from 12 months to 6 months. The impact was immediate with a new broader range of customers attracted to the new higher limits at lower interest than unsecured loans. This was certainly a key achievement for the NPA.

Miltons of Liverpool

The Magazine

Another victim of the decline of Pawnbroking was the weekly Pawnbrokers Gazette. The last ever edition was number 6303 at the end of 1958. It had been printed every week from October 1838 to December 1958. It was succeeded by the NPA Journal which was published until 1986. This was printed monthly at first, then bi-monthly and then quarterly. It was replaced by the Pawnbroker Times and then The Pawnbroker Magazine in 2006 which is still in print today.

1960 Act and NPA

By the late 1950's as noted in the previous chapter, with the introduction of the welfare state no pawnbroker was making much money. In many case clerical costs of servicing pawns outweighed the interest value of them. Something had to be done. The 1960 Act resulted from the very hard work of the National Pawnbrokers Association who drafted the Act from 1955 and submitted it to the Select Committee to review. When presented as a bill to parliament it passed through parliament and became in Act in 13 weeks flat. The principal benefit was the raising of the amount of loan on one pawn ticket from £10 to £50.

Sale of Lombard House

In 1973 another victim of the downturn in pawnbroking was the NPAs headquarters at Lombard House. The NPA owned the 5 floor plus basement building but effectively barely used one floor and rented the rest out. It was in need of significant repair and the authorities wanted to make a compulsory purchase in order to develop the area. Fearing a rock bottom price, the NPA Council resolved to sell the land and 5 storey building to developers privately for a sum of £210,000. In 2016 a one bedroom flat in the area would cost £1 million. The furniture including the board room table was given to Harvey & Thompson.

The NPA was subsequently administered from the home of Mr Brown, the general secretary, in Southend-on-Sea, and then subsequently from offices at 6 Wimpole Street, from Fleet St, from

Caversham in Reading, and currently resides back on Fleet St at number 107.

Input into the Consumer Credit Act

Perhaps the most significant moment in the history of the NPA was the passing of the Consumer Credit Act. As we have seen in the previous chapter, the NPA Council lobbied hard, carried out it's own pre-research and made a submission to Parliament, primarily to increase the amount that could be pawned on one ticket or contract. The Government chose to bring Acts affecting pawnbrokers and moneylenders all under one Act focusing on consumer credit and have one department of government overseeing this. Again the NPA had shown that working as a committee and engaging directly with Government, they were able to influence the outcome.

The Consumer Credit Directive of 2010 was the first occasion when the NPA had not been an active part of shaping legislation. As discussed in the previous chapter, the NPA were not alone in assuming the provisions would not apply to pawnbroking. The impact as we have seen was dramatic with the advent of the APR calculation and the SECCI pre contract information. The NPAs response was late but effective with two hastily organised events with lawyers presenting the impact of the law on members' activities, admirably put together by then CEO Des Milligan. The NPA also brought together the main software providers and explained exactly what was required in terms of changes to contracts and the APR calculations. These were swiftly implemented and the profession entered a new era with the incoming CEO myself, Ray Perry, dealing with the compliance from 2012 onwards.

From 2014 the Government announced the new Financial Conduct Authority regime that the industry would be under. The NPA worked closely with the new authority and the author, Ray Perry, was part of the Treasury Committee working group to implement the change over. NPA specifically worked with them on the drafting of relevant pawnbroking sections. As well as abiding by the rules as enacted, this placed the additional burden on the firm of having to comply with processes, systems and requirements really designed for large corporations. Most of the industry did not understand the terms and jargon written by compliance managers for compliance managers. However to their credit by the time most were invited to apply for full permissions with the FCA in March 2016, the majority had completed the bureaucracy due in no short measure to the resources provided by the NPA for it's members. The NPA only lost a handful of members as a result. These were mainly jewellers who decided the small amount of business generated from pawns did not warrant all the bureaucracy.

Perhaps the most important benefit was that agreement was reached that pawnbroking would be exempted from the requirement to carry out full creditworthiness checks as common sense dictated that the pawn was the security for the loan and therefore was in itself the credit check. FCA agreed but decided that if a full credit check had not been undertaken the pawnbroker would not be allowed to chase debt beyond the value of the goods when sold. In reality pawnbrokers had not chased debts anyway for the practical reason that if the customer couldn't afford to redeem they are unlikely to have other assets worth chasing. One side effect however, was that where a debt existed and the pawn didn't cover the debt but part payments had been made, then the part payments must be returned to the customer. This is a moot point because one could argue that the part payments were a contribution to the debt incurred. However the FCAs ruling was that a customer who hadn't made a part payment would not have to make it once the pawn had been sold so why should someone who had been good enough to make a payment be penalised compared to the person who had made no payments.

The Banking Issue

Ever since the 2008 financial crisis for the banking sector there had been an increasing unwillingness to open new bank current accounts for money lenders. Some banks would open accounts for pawnbrokers but not money service businesses, defined as those transferring money, providing foreign currency or cashing cheques. Unfortunately the NPA establish through member research that 72 per cent of pawnbrokers were also money service businesses. Traditionally, fearing the worst, most pawnbrokers had opened current accounts with a number of banks but by 2014 some 91% were down to their last account. The reason most citied by banks was compliance cost for them in servicing account because of Anti Money Laundering regulations imposed by the Financial Action Task Force (representing 35 major countries), US Regulation and HMRC rules. This effectively acted as a market barrier to entry since 2015 and has yet to be resolved. The NPA are working with the FCA,

Treasury, British Bankers Association, other kindred bodies, and interestingly the NPA in America, a separate organisation with the same name, to try to resolve this issue.

The Future

The NPA has been very busy in recent times helping and guiding members in the unchartered waters of compliance and more recently the banking issues. The NPA is currently extremely relevant but must continue to be so in this increasingly legislative environment, and members must remain relevant to their customers. There will always be a need to service short term secured loans and the Association must continue to push forward the benefits of pawnbroking.

The modern Council is made up of 14 member seats. The top 6 fee payers, called Corporate members, get a free seat. The other 8 are elected. Since 2015 2 are required to stand down but can be re-elected by member vote. Any member can stand for election.

The Council of the NPA in 2016 comprised of;

President	Paul Smit, Cashbrokers
Deputy President	Nathan Finch, Pickwick
Treasurer	Mark Sumpter, Cheques and Change
Margot Walker	Former President, W J Edwards
Haywood Milton	Miltons of Liverpool
David Page	The Gold Emporium
Jim Tannahill	Hopkins and Jones
Stephen Dexter	Fish Brothers
John Nichols, CEO	H&T, Corporate
Peter Kenyon, CEO	Ramsdens, Corporate
Martyn Jenkins, CEO	Cash Converters, Corporate
Paul Court, MD	Axcess Group (Cash Generator and Cheque Centre) Corporate
Stuart Howard, MD	The Money Shop, Corporate
Sanjiv Corepal, CEO	Albemarle and Bond, Corporate

Dignitaries of the NPA.

PRESIDENTS		
NAME	TO	FROM
Alderman John Goolden JP Mayor of Newcastle	1892	1895
Henry Arther Attenborough JP	1895	1913
Walter Bull	1913	1925
Sidney Smith	1925	1931
Frederick Ohlson	1931	1940
James Smellie	1940	1941
A E Thomson	1941	1946
Edgar Bowes	1946	1949
William H Dawson	1949	1958
W J D Porritt	1958	1966
A D Cook	1966	1967
E T Brown	1968	1970
C Suttenstall	1970	1980
H S Wilkins	1980	1986
J D G Cook	1986	1990
L C Watson	1990	1991
John Milton	1991	1995
Brian T K Edwards	1995	2001
Phil P Murphy	2001	2004
John Nichols	2004	2009
W Josh Fish	2009	2011
Ms Margot Walker	2011	2014
Paul Smit	2014	present

VICE-PRESIDENTS		
NAME	TO	FROM
A A George	1899	1901
Stanley J Attenborough	1904	1910
C J Thompson	1910	1915
R Harold Attenborough	1916	1931
John Long	1931	1937
James Smellie	1937	1940
Edgar Bowes	1941	1946
A E Thomson	1946	1949
W R Amos	1949	1953
L G Norris	1953	1958
E T Brown	1958	1968
C Suttenstall	1968	1970
S J Davies	1970	1972
H S Wilkins	1972	1980
J D G Cook	1980	1986
Lewis C Watson	1986	1990
John Milton	1990	1991
E P Ireland	1991	1993
Brian T K Edwards	1993	1995
Vince P Way	1995	1999
Phil P Murphy	1999	2001
Jim Tannahill	2011	2004
W Josh Fish	2004	2007
Margot Walker	2007	2009
David Page	2009	2010
Nathan Finch	2010	Present

TREASURERS		
NAME	TO	FROM
J Ashridge Telfer	1892	1895
Walter Bull	1895	1913
C H Bingemann	1913	1931
Robert Starling	1931	1941
W R Amos	1941	1949
L G Norris	1949	1953
E T Brown	1953	1958
S J Davies	1958	1970
H S Wilkins	1970	1972
F E Roberts	1972	1981
J S A Harris	1981	1986
E P Ireland	1986	1991
R A Bragg	1991	1997
W Josh Fish	1997	2003
Eddie F A Ford	2003	2007
M Lemmon	2007	2009
Jim Tannahill	2009	2011
Helen Reed	2012	2013
Mark Sumpter	2013	Present

HONORARY SECRETARIES		
NAME	TO	FROM
Alfred Hardaker	1892	1895
James Sprunt	1895	1900
C J Thompson	1900	1910
Walter Bull	1910	1912
Sidney Smith	1913	1921
F K Ohlson	1921	1931
P Davies	1931	1937
B G Paul	1937	1941

GENERAL SECRETARIES		
NAME	TO	FROM
B G Paul	1941	1953
J E Brown	1953	1982
W A Routledge	1982	1985
J S Roscoe	1985	1987
Tim G Ford	1988	1991

SECRETARY GENERAL/CHIEF EXECUTIVE		
NAME	TO	FROM
Tim G Ford	1991	2006
Des Milligan	2006	2011
Ray K Perry	2012	Present

ASSISTANT SECRETARIES		
NAME	TO	FROM
John Attenborough	1913	1926
Charles A Oak	1925	1941
J E Brown	1949	1953
H Bell-Roberts	1991	2000
Nathan J Finch	2001	2006

Chapter 7 The UK Market and the Future

Research from Apex[29] in 2015, quotes research from the Joseph Rowntree Foundation showing that 51% of loans were for day to day items, and a further 27% were for household bills. It points out that people used pawnbrokers generally because of their proximity 53% or by recommendation 19%. It generally tends to be the same people using pawnbrokers over again and that they are highly satisfied with the service[30] , a level of 78% satisfaction was recorded. The traditional market is just 3% of the population. A significant factor in this choice is that an estimated 8 million people do not have bank accounts and many see the pawnbroker as their 'bank'. The number of bank branches fell from 14,000 to 9,700 from 2004 to 1015, such that there are fewer branches per capita in the UK than any other state in Europe or America. At the same time number of credit cards issued fell from 73 to 56.9 million.

Growth since 2010 has come from loans to small businesses for cashflow purposes and from higher end middle class loans of designer items through fims such as Sutton and Robertsons, Atpledge, Prestige Pawnbrokers, and Posh Pawn Brokers.

---

[29] Pawnbrokers and High Street Loan Stores 2015, Apex Insights
[30] Bristol Report 2011, The NPA

Much of this growth has been partly influenced by two very successful Channel 4 series (by Boomerang Productions) called Posh Pawn and Posh Pawnbrokers. This sector also includes designer and high end watches and includes for example, Miltons of Liverpool, who are Rolex experts.

The key online firm is Borro who dominate this sector of pawnbroking. However, for most pawnbrokers the online presence is mainly for the sale of second hand goods, or as a signpost to pawnbroking. In general customers like to 'eye ball' the pawnbroker and consider handing over a family heirloom, for example, as a matter of trust whereby they want to see the pawnbroker and check security is in place.

The market grew to £936,000 loan value by 2012 but has declined since to around £700,000. This was because the gold price fell by 30% in 2013 meaning that not so much could be leant against jewellery items. The gold price peaked at £1,125 per ounce in 2011. By March 2016 in was £883 (-22%) so it has recently made a small recovery.

As a result of this turbulence many of the larger pawnbrokers have cut back their number of stores. Between Albemarle and Bond, Cheque Centre, Cash Generator and The Money Shop, over 500 stores closed between 2012 and 2015. By 2016 The Money Shop had the most stores, whereas the largest traditional store was H&T Pawnbrokers with 191 stores, with northern based Ramsdens as the second largest followed by A&B. The largest of the generalists is

Cash Converters who sell second hand goods as well as offering pawnbroking. NPA statistics show that of its 170 members, 75% of its members stores are owned by just 6 companies. However, unlike some other retail markets it is still possible to find at least one independent in most UK towns.

Compared to America, the UK market is about 15% of the size, with some 10,000 stores reported across the USA. However, the UK industry has a much higher average loan- between £250 and £400 in the UK and about $150 (£105) in the US.

According to Apex, most pawnbrokers margins were between 5% and 15%, although most stores would enhance their pawnbroking return with other activities such as money service businesses activities including foreign exchange, cheque cashing and money transfer. In addition many would sell second hand jewellery, and other second hand products. The may also buy items in with an option for the customer to buy them back in 28 days at a higher price.

With the fall in gold price and the increase in compliance and bureaucracy as a result of Financial Conduct Authority regime coming in to force in 2015, it had been assumed that the number of pawnbrokers might fall. However, in reality only a handful of members of the NPA resigned and the FCA have not rejected any members known to the Association.

The Main Pawnbrokers

The Money Shop

This company is part of Dollar Finance Group and was acquired in April 2014 by Lone Star a US private equity firm for $1.3 billion. The same group also owns traditional up market pawnbroker Suttons and Robertsons, which is primarily London based. The latter will take pawn loans of up to £1 million. Globally pawnbroking loans represent 9% of their business. According to 2013 accounts nearly 50% of their turnover comes from the UK. In 2014 the Money Shop generated £154 million in revenue which was a drop of 17%. Overall it made a loss of £61 million in 2014 and consequently rationalised its number of stores.

H&T

By 2014, the group had £88m turnover from 191 stores. The
business was started by Walter Harvey and Charles James Thompson
in 1897. The business built up to 26 stores by 1992, when it was
acquired by Cash America Inc, the second largest American
pawnbroking chain. However, in September 2004 a management
team led by John Nichols with funds from Rutland Partners
undertook a buy-out for £49m. In May 2006, it achieved an AIM
listing with market capitalisation around £60m. They have a pledge
book of around £39 million.

Axcess Group

The firm trades as Cheque Centre and Cash Generator. By 2013 combined revenue was £405 million. They had to make significant adjustments to their business to meet FCA compliance requirements during 2014 and 2015. During this time they downsized their pawnbroking store portfolio. Pawnbroking loans now account for around 2% of their turnover.

Albemarle and Bond (A&B)

A&B was established in Bristol in 1983. The firm was previously listed on the AIM market reaching capitalisation of £220m and shares worth £2. It delisted in 2014 at a value of just £4m. Efforts to improve performance failed leading turn around the business proved unsuccessful, and led to the company filing for bankruptcy in March 2014. Shares were suspended at 6.65p. The company lost over 60% of its value in just 3 days. The assets were sold to Promethean Investments in 2015. These asstes included 128 branches with 628 employees. The fund raised £150m from institutions for investing in special situation companies and the first deal was backed by US private equity group Apollo, which bought up the A&B"s debts. In November 2015 Asia Growth Capital of Singapore acquired A&B/ Speedloan Finance for £26.5m. Pawnbroking accounted for 62% of A&B"s business in 2015.

Cash Converters

The firm was set up in Perth, Western Australia, in 1984 by Brian Cumins. They have nearly 700 stores in 20 countries. It is listed on the Australian Stock Exchange. They started trading in the UK in 1992. By 2014, pawnbroking accounted for 7.2% of its global revenue. In 2009 EZCorp the US pawnbroker bought a 30% stake. UK accounts for 30% of the group at £55 million by 2013. Cash Converters now has 217 UK stores, 166 of which are franchised. Turnover increased to nearly £35 million by 2014. Pawnbroking represents about 4.5% of their business.

Ramsdens

The firm is based primarily in the north of England, Scotland and Wales and had a turnover of £42 million in 2014, of which approximately 12% was from pawnbroking activities. At this time the company had 127 stores. The company was privately owned by its management until September 2014 when it was backed by private equity fund, NorthEdge Capital.

Borro

Borro is the UK"s largest online pawnbroker based on Chancery Lane , London, and focuses on the top end loan market, typically above £10,000 and will take pawns on cars, fine art, watches and collections. They will lend up to £2 million and were set up in the US in 2012. The firm was founded by Paul Aitken, in 2008. By 2013 they had a revenue of £10.3 million but made a loss of £9.9 million. In February 2015, Borro achieved £13 million of funding from OurCrowd from Israel and Rocket Internet of Germany. The primary reason was to expand into South America and Asia, and attract peer to peer lending to fund loans. In total the company has raised in excess of $200m, in debt and equity financing rounds. It raised $112m from Victory Park Capital in 2013.

Other Independents

The largest non Corporate status member is Cashbrokers which has a chain of multiple franchise businesses involved in pawnbroking , buying and selling, as well as money service business activities. They operate around the country with a base in Grantham. The Cash Shop have a number of stores based in the Midlands.

The largest traditional Pawnbroker is Fish Brothers who have a chain of stores across London and the South East. Pickwick Pawnbrokers have a slightly smaller chain of stores across south London and Kent.

Miltons of Liverpool and other Miltons stores, focus on upmarket jewellery and pawnbroking in the North West

The Overall market make up

2016 Pawnbroking Stores

1 store only	127
2- 5 stores	37
6-10 stores	10
11-50	6
51-360	6

The Future

Pawnbroking has weathered recent storms successfully and will continue to part of everyday life for millions of people as it has been for at least 3,000 years, very few have stopped trading because of the gold price, bureaucracy or competition. Pawnbroking continues to be a relatively small sub bullion pound, thriving sector, highly regarded by its customers, by the regulators and for example by the former Governor of the Bank Of England Mervyn King[31] who states;

> "Central banks must behave more like pawnbrokers to stamp out recklessness…..It is time to replace the lender of last resort (the central banks) by the pawnbroker for all seasons"

Hopefully in my time at the National Pawnbrokers Association 2012 to 2016 I have at least started the progression towards much better

---

[31] The End Of Alchemy, Mervyn King 2016

acceptance and recognition of this unique, interesting and crucial market place. In the future as the trusted relationship between the pawnbroker and customers continues to mature and more customers turn to pawnbrokers we should see a growth in small and medium sized businesses using pawnbrokers. The type of pawn will become more varied from designer handbags to cars and memorabilia, and the pawn loan will stand on its own merit as a viable option competing with banks and other forms of loan. It is likely that that the pawnbroking model in the UK will spread across Europe as governments note that pawnbroking is reliable, customer friendly and relatively low interest. The pawnbroker is highly regulated and is playing his role in the growth of society and will do so for the foreseeable future working with regulators and government.

Appendix   Questions and Answers

The Consumer Credit Act 1974, the Consumer Credit Directive 2010(EU), and the rules of the Financial Conduct Authority have debatably created a sometimes bewildering scenario for customers to understand. Here are some popular questions and answers;

Q) If a pawn is not redeemed what notification letters or communication are sent to the customer?

A) If the pawn was for less than £75 and was on a 6 month contract, then the item becomes the pawnbrokers. No notifications are sent and any profit is kept by the pawnbroker. If the pawn was for less than £75 but was on a 7 month contract, the title of the goods remains with the customer and they will be noitified after sale has been made and will receive any profit after loan, interest and reasonable costs.

The law states that if the pledge loan was for £100 or more the pawnbroker must give the customer 14 days' notice of intention to sell.

However, when the items are sold a Results of Sale letter must be sent for any item where the pledge loan was £75 or more. So if the customer ,for example, had taken a loan of say £80, they are not required to be told that the item was going to be sold, but must be told when its sold.

Q) I have been offered a one month sale and buy back agreement is the pawnbroking?

A) No it isn't. This kind of transaction is a normal sale agreement under Contract Law in which you are given an option to buy the item back 28 days later at a higher price. These contracts are not covered by the Consumer Credit Act and are considered general contracts whereby the title to the goods is immediately sold with an option to buy back. The consumer is not protected in the same way as a pawnbroking agreement would protect them and there is no redress. If anything goes wrong you would have to take civil action yourself against the shopkeeper which might prove expensive.

Q) I don't understand what the APR means, how do I know if it's a good deal?

A) Obviously comparing one APR with other competitor's APRs is one way, however the best way may simply be to look at the monthly interest rate quoted, so if you borrow £100 at 6% and redeem at say the end of month 3 you would have to pay back £118. However you do need to give a months notice of intention to redeem early because you are breaking the contract. If you do want the item back immediately most pawnbrokers will allow this but you may be asked to pay up to 28 days interest penalty because you have broken the contract.

Q) What would happen to my pawned jewellery if the Pawnbroker went into liquidation?

A) Firstly it is highly unlikely for a pawnbroker to go out of business. In the event of liquidation the customer still has title and rights, and the following would happen;

- if the company is bought, the pawns continue, and the existing contract is still valid

- 2) if it goes bust/ the receiver would ensure that the contract continues, although they may offer an incentive / discount to redeem early. The customer would however, not have the right to renew the pawn contract.

In practice the pawnbroker is likely to sell his 'book' to a nearby pawnbroker. In all eventualities the customer would be informed where their item is to be stored and where to go to redeem it.

Q) Can say a husband redeem an article pawned by his wife?

A)   Under no circumstances can a pawnbroker release the item without the express permission of pledger. The pledge was taken in good faith and she has confirmed by signing the contract that she is the owner of the item. If this is not the case the onus is on the husband's solicitor to prove this to the police and court. Otherwise it would be illegal to release the item without a solicitor's letter (affidavit).

Under the original Pawnbroking Acts of 1800 and 1872 finding a pawn ticket was like winning the lottery, you could just go and redeem whatever the pawn was. This has not been the case in more recent times. Section 117(1) of the Consumer Credit Act provides that 'on surrender of the pawn-receipt, and payment of the amount owing...the pawnee shall deliver the pawn to the bearer of the pawn receipt'. However, this is subject to section 117(2) which states 'subsection (1) does not apply is the pawnee knows or has reasonable cause to suspect that the bearer of the pawn-receipt is neither the owner of the pawn nor authorised by the owner to redeem it'.

 Further, to redeem in these circumstances would breach Treating Customers Fairly principles under FCA Rules and potentially could amount to money laundering (if the pawnbroker knows or suspects that the bearer of the pawn-receipt has acquired it illegally, which must be the case here where the circumstances suggest theft or fraud).

The principle in terms of redemption, realization or any other matter pertaining to the contract, is that unless the pawnbroker is satisfied that the party in question is the owner of the pawn or is authorised by the owner to redeem it then you should not allow it. 'Authorisation' in this context should be taken to mean a clear and unequivocal statement by the original pawnor, in writing, that the pawnbroker is authorised to deal with a named third party in respect of the contract.

Q) A couple who are divorcing have amicably agreed to pawn a valuable ring as they both need to release funds to pay their respective solicitors. Can they put both their names on the contract, and both sign?

A) Only one person should sign as the designated owner and one address should be used.

Q) Can I literally pawn anything?

A) Pretty much, yes. The pawn is security against a loan so it is all a matter of trust between the customer and pawnbroker. The pawnbroker is taking all the risk that you may never return but often a pawnbroker may be happy to provide a higher loan to a regular customer because he trusts the person. In terms of what you can pawn, well you could pawn your classic car collection, helicopter, antiques, fine wine collection, designer handbags or anything with perceived value except for land which has different rules more akin to a mortgage. You can't pawn live fire arms, or live animals, perishable food or humans!

Q) Can I make part payments during the contract term?

A) Yes. This will reduce the total debt from the day you make the payment and the interest will continue to be charged on the remaining balance.

Q) If I can't redeem my pawn how do I know it will be sold for a good price?

A) The pawnbroker is legally bound to get the best price he can for the customer when he sells the item. This is obviously down to getting the true market value on the day. The pawnbroker will know from experience whether this would be through auction, by selling in the window, or in some cases through scrapping an item for its gold value. However , the true second value is often different to a jewellers valuation for insurance purposes which is often a higher value of replacing the item with its brand new equivalent.

Q) Can a pawn be for less than 6 months?

A) You can redeem a pawn at any time on any day and pay interest to that date only plus a penalty if you have not given notice. Pawns tend to be for at least 6 months contractually, but some pawnbrokers do offer a shorter period. The problem is that legally the pawn cannot be sold until the 6 months period is up, so if the contract were say 4 months and the item was not redeemed you would have to wait an extra few months before the pawnbroker can sell the item and you can get any profit back.

Printed in Poland
by Amazon Fulfillment
Poland Sp. z o.o., Wrocław